What It Means to Be Human

Made In the Image of God

SMYTH&HELWYS
PUBLISHING, INCORPORATED   MACON, GEORGIA

What It Means to Be Human

Made In the Image of God

Molly T. Marshall

SMYTH&
HELWYS

Smyth & Helwys Publishing, Inc.
6316 Peake Road
Macon, Georgia 31210-3960
1-800-747-3016
© 1995, 2001 by Smyth & Helwys Publishing
All rights reserved.
Printed in the United States of America.

The paper used in this publication meets the minimum
requirements of American Standard for Information
Sciences—Permanence of paper for Printed Library Materials.
ANSI Z39.48-1984.

Library of Congress Cataloging-in-Publication Data

Marshall, Molly Truman.
    What it means to be human / by Molly T. Marshall.
    pp. cm.
    1. Man (Christian theology)
    I. Title
    BT701.2.M3568 1995
    233—dc20   94-41124
                                    CIP

ISBN 1-57312-352-8

Cor ad cor loquitur
Heart speaketh unto heart

Contents

Preface

The late Jim Henson's beloved star "muppet," Kermit the Frog, is known for his saying, "It's not easy being green." Well, as you and I have discovered along the way, "It's not easy being human," either. This book is an invitation to spend some time trying to discover why being human poses so much promise and remains so perplexing for us.

We as reflective creaturely beings try to make sense of our lives, which means that at some point we ask, "What does it mean to be human?" It is part of our identity, as persons made in the image of God, to question the meaning of our lives. I hope that in these pages you will hear some of your own questions and find some direction toward the answer as we explore together some of the dimensions of our humanity.

I have written these brief chapters out of the firm conviction that God has blessed human beings by giving us a unique dignity and purpose in this world. As God's creatures, we have a vocation and a destiny that relates us to all of creation as well as to the Gracious Creator who called us into being. I believe that it is a good thing to be human and that a disciplined Christian faith requires that we examine our lives.

In this study, we will reflect upon many questions about our human origins and our relationship to God, our work and our play, human relationships in marriage, family, and community, what it means to be a male or a female human being, God's purpose of redemption in light of suffering and death, and the hope that can sustain us even in the midst of the difficulties in life.

Perhaps these questions can encourage you to raise others, for surely we are complex creatures who cannot be summed up by a simple explanation.

I do not write as an "expert," but as a companion on the journey of faith. None of us can continue in faith alone. We need the encouragement of others and the wisdom they have gleaned through their attempts to integrate their joys and griefs into the tapestry of belief that is uniquely theirs. Thus, I have shared some of my own pilgrimage in faith as well as vignettes of those persons who have taught me about what it means to be human.

Many sources can shed light on our common humanity, yet I have looked to the Bible chiefly because I believe that it offers the testimony of persons whose lives have been touched uniquely by God. It continues to provide insight and direction for those of us far removed from the historical setting in which it was written, and I have tried to present its stories and teachings in such a way that we might hear them afresh in our own cultural context. I will also draw upon contemporary anthropological, sociological, psychological, and theological studies because they, too, have much to offer toward understanding what it means to be human.

I earnestly desire that this study will allow each of us a new gratitude to God for the wonder of our human identity and new perspectives on how to actualize more fully that calling as committed Christians. Many other interpretations of what it means to be human compete for our attention; thus we must know "the reason for the hope that is within us" (1 Pet 3:15). I trust that the reader will be blessed by new insight even as the author has been blessed in the process of reflection and writing.

I want to express gratitude to Princeton Theological Seminary for naming me a Visiting Scholar during my sabbatical, which allowed time to study, write, walk, and enjoy the grace of becoming more fully human. Thanks also to my beloved colleagues (both present and former) at The Southern Baptist Theological

Seminary for sustaining friendship through it all. Finally, special thanks are due Peggy Shaw for her meticulous care in helping prepare the final manuscript.

Epiphany 1995
Louisville, Kentucky

Becoming Human: A Life's Work

In your travels, you have probably accumulated a collection of pictures or other keepsakes to help you remember the distinctive culture and character of the places you have visited. A picture of the Sphinx, a tiny piece of wedgewood, an olive wood carving, or a delicate porcelain vase will each undoubtedly bring to mind a flood of impressions and reflections on past visits to many places.

The strongest memories I carry from my travels, however, relate to the persons I have met. The wonderful strands of colors and accents that weave the tapestry of humanity are stunning in their complexity and common simplicity. Let me introduce you to some of these persons I carry in my heart.

While working as a campus minister in Jerusalem several years ago, I came to know three young Arab women from Nazareth who were attending Hebrew University. They included me in their trips home, and on one occasion they invited me to attend a family wedding in their Orthodox church. There is no better opportunity to learn about a different culture! Our animated conversations took many twists and turns as we explored our common concerns for peace and social justice. They shared with me their passionate desire to take full advantage of their educational opportunity, which is still a rather uncommon venture for women in their culture. I grew to love them and the war-torn, divided country I had been privileged to see through their eyes.

Later as a graduate student in England, I became acquainted with the Grisanti family who ran a small Italian restaurant near my flat. The restaurant was really a family business with mother and father, brothers and sisters all involved in shopping, cooking, arranging flowers on the tables, and serving their enticing dishes. Perhaps I looked both hungry and lonely—whatever—they sensed my need and readily took me in. Dinner with them became a regular occurrence two or three nights a week, and it was a real treat after my regular fare of instant leek or oxtail soup prepared in a tea kettle in my room.

Often they commiserated with me "being so far from home" and cut off from my family and friends. Obviously they were feeling the same kind of distance from their roots as I was, for they spoke frequently of the things they missed in Italy. The English "simply do not know how to grow tomatoes," they would complain. When an earthquake hit the small Italian village where the majority of their family still lived, the tragedy drew us closer together as I expressed concern for them. As they allowed me to enter into the pain of their extended family, we realized our relationship as a part of the one human family. I recall so well eating my last dinner in Cambridge with the Grisantis before saying a reluctant good-bye.

During that semester in England, I also developed a friendship with Alice, a young woman from South Africa. None of the reports I had read of the racial violence that accompanied apartheid could compare with her first-hand accounts of attending mixed-race student gatherings that had been broken up by the police. Because of her activities promoting inclusive Bible study groups while a student in Durban, she was listed as "politically suspicious." She lived in constant fear that her mail would be intercepted and tampered with before she could receive it. She knew that her bold stand for justice might well create a paper trail that would haunt her.

During one trip together across the channel for a few days on the continent, I had ample opportunity to feel her tension. Holding a South African passport subjected Alice to intense scrutiny and scorn at every border; her protests that she was working to abolish apartheid had little effect on the calloused border guards.

I came to share my friend's anxieties about the future as she planned to continue working for racial justice as a professor in a primarily black university. She was convinced that education was the only way to break down the racial stereotypes that kept the overwhelming majority of South Africans under oppression, robbing them of their human dignity.

Now, as I write, I am on sabbatical leave and am studying at Princeton Theological Seminary in New Jersey. This small town of Princeton is teeming with people from all around the world. It is my turn now to extend hospitality to these international students who find themselves in an alien culture that is drastically different from anything they have known. In one way or another they are all terribly alone as they struggle to cope with the complexities of our culture, including strange food, confusing speech, and in some instances, forms of dress that seem strange and awkward. In this setting I am once again keenly aware of our cultural differences, while at the same time, I am acutely conscious of the common concerns we all share as humans inhabiting the earth.

One Humanity Expressed in Diverse Cultures

This leads me to ask, "What does it mean to be human?" As I reflect on persons I have met while traveling and those who intersect my life daily, I see patterns of behavior characteristic to the human family that offer tell-tale clues to our identity. Through the perceptive skill of anthropologists, we are learning that these patterns find their shape in connection with human needs and what is involved in satisfying them.[1]

First, we all tend to assume that the culture in which we were raised is "normal." The father of a friend of mine displays "Archie Bunker" attitudes about most things. This was glaringly evident when my friend and his father flew to Germany. Upon landing in Frankfurt, the passengers were herded into two lines to clear customs: one for "nationals" and one for "foreigners." My friend's father loudly complained about such a distinction, reminding everyone that he "ain't no foreigner!" To be sure, family ties and homeland form our images of reality, and we tend to measure all that is new and unfamiliar by these images.[2]

Second, we long for acceptance and understanding; yet we come to realize that the price for receiving these gifts is determined, in a way, by how much of ourselves we are willing to give to others. This giving requires great patience and willingness to attend to social customs that may feel quite awkward to us at first—or always. Yet, respect for the distinctiveness of other persons is crucial because our human dignity is always expressed in a cultural wrapping.

I remember well the first time I visited Nazareth with my Arab student friends. While I am sure they tried to prepare me, I was far from ready to meet the expectations they had for me as their guest. I soon learned that to be polite, I was expected to dance at the party held the night before the wedding—with whomever was brave enough to ask. My inept efforts were a comic witness to the fact that I had been one of the faithful few who abstained from the sin of dancing at the small Christian university where I received my degree!

But there was more. I was expected to visit in the homes of all of their relatives. Each visit included looking at all the wedding and funeral pictures of various family members while munching on some fattening sweet prepared especially for my visit. Of course, it would have been a breach of good manners to refuse anything. When I returned to Jerusalem after my long weekend, I was literally exhausted and several pounds heavier. I made no secret about being irritated with "their ways" as I crossly compared them with "how we do things back home." My provincial attitude and presumed cultural "superiority" stood out in bold relief for everyone to see and hear. "Culture shock" really does exist. All of us retain more xenophobia than we would care to admit.

Third, all human beings strive for security, both physically and emotionally. Obviously, these twin concerns can hardly be separated.[3] Recently our world has experienced the travesty of thousands of refugees lined up on the Iraqui-Jordanian border. Displaced, discouraged, and outraged, they have been reduced to scrambling for basic necessities of life: water, bread, and shelter. They protest that they "feel less than human." Many persons have left professions behind that in no way prepared them for the animal-like competition they face simply to survive. These displaced refugees are living under great personal threats, including the potential loss of economic security; separation from family and friends; a feeling of abandonment by their countries of origin; and, of course, fear of death through disease, dehydration, or military attack.

While we as humans display a phenomenal ability to adapt to graphically different climates, living spaces, and diets, living without a measure of personal security wounds the spirit and diminishes hope. I recently saw a bitterly ironic cartoon in the *New York Times* that depicted four young men—one Hispanic, one Anglo, two African-Americans—wearily sitting on a street corner complaining that urban renewal would soon claim their "corner office" where they regularly "hang out." Their shrugs of resignation made it clear that they did not expect anything but disappointment, anyway.

Faced with the daily struggle for survival, persons such as these find difficulty in giving any attention to more complex cultural and spiritual needs. Their preoccupation with food and shelter leaves them little time for anything else. As the studies of the psychologist Abraham Maslow have demonstrated, human beings must first take care of basic physical needs before they can pursue other concerns. Maslow devised the "hierarchy of needs," a ladder that portrays the order of priority of the needs of human beings. We are often critical of certain races or economic levels (or even the female gender) for not producing great thinkers or artists. If we follow Maslow's reasoning, however, it is foolish to expect persons to be concerned about the "higher needs" when their basic ones go unmet.

I am convinced that many persons live such an insecure existence physically that they live in a state of denial or escapism concerning their emotional needs. Thus, they live in the clutches of continual drug abuse, numbing television addiction, or, in the case of a growing number, more violent expressions of their frustrations. Many civic leaders are currently warning that racial hostility is on the rise; it appears to be a way of venting deep-seated resentment over the systemic poverty and life on the margins that many experience in our society.[4]

Obviously, we humans need more than just those things that sustain physically, but in the absence of these, there is no will or energy to pursue other concerns. Indeed, often the struggle for survival becomes so all consuming that the deeper questions of the human spirit are suffocated. Tragically, this denial and suffocation can also occur in the lives of those with plenty; the insistent pressure to "consume" that marks western culture leaves such people still empty because they have not understood the deeper questions about the meaning and purpose of their lives and the accompanying spiritual needs.[5]

The writer of John's Gospel gave us the marvelous scene in the synagogue at Capernaum in which Jesus acknowledged the necessity of devoting effort to obtaining physical or "perishable bread" essential to sustaining life (John 6). At the same time, though, he stressed the deeper need for "living bread," which will satisfy the deepest hunger for life with meaning. Here, as in the Sermon on the Mount, Jesus assured those who would follow him that true life consists of more than what we shall eat or drink or wear (Matt 6). Thus, deeper hunger can only be satisfied by God, the creator and sustainer of the universe.[6]

The Mystery of Human Existence

In the Victorian era, the art of "making introductions" was an elaborate ritual of pomp and protocol. The gracious host or hostess needed to make sure that the ranking guests were presented in just the right manner, with proper acknowledgment of titles, degrees, and family connections. Only after being "properly introduced" could a person feel free to engage in polite conversation with the other guests.

Our modern day, characterized by the informality of first names and casual conversation, still retains something of the demeanor of this more formal era. We still politely introduce people who have not met each other so they can feel relaxed and move on to a meaningful conversation and relationship. Usually these introductions include the person's name and profession.

Yet, we are all too well aware how little we really know of another person if we only know his or her name and vocation. So in the "small talk" that follows, we usually attempt to find other common links with such questions as "Where are you from?" "Where did you receive your schooling?" "How long have you lived here?" "Who is your family?" At the conclusion of this get acquainted conversation, if it seems to have been mutually pleasing, we may feel we have found a new friend, but even with what we have learned in our initial meeting, the mystery of the other person has scarcely been penetrated.

Students of literature and history speak of the "narrative quality" of human life.[7] To really know another person, we must listen carefully to his or her "story." To know myself, I must have a sense of the major passages of my life and be able to connect them meaningfully.

Each of us desperately desires to be known; to be a stranger is most uncomfortable, as you know if you have ever moved, changed schools, or had an extended stay away from home. Yet, few of us know ourselves well enough to introduce ourselves fully to someone else. Unfortunately, many of us are strangers to ourselves as well as to others. We tell a few self-descriptive facts, as if what we own or how we earn our living or where we went to school somehow summarizes our twenty or forty or seventy years of life. We are left, however, with a haunting feeling that there is really more to us than that, more than, perhaps, we even know. The nature of our own humanity often remains a mystery.[8]

Who Am I?

The human being has been described as the one who relentlessly questions self. Who of us has not asked "Why did I do that?" "Where am I going?" "Can I make it through this?" "What do I matter?" These questions shape much of our striving, even if they remain at a subconscious level. As the early church father, Augustine, wrote in his *Confessions*: "I have become a question to myself. I have become a land of weariness to myself" (10.16.25). In his struggle to understand his motives and actions, Augustine had become a riddle even to himself.

Those of us who strive to be self-aware can well identify with Augustine's frustration. We question ourselves at every turn, for we long to know who we truly are. The answers to the basic human questions do not seem to be readily available simply on the evidence of life as we experience it. Consequently, we do not seem to have the ability to stop asking "why" even in the most numbing circumstances.[9]

At the same time, the law courts and news media and doctors' offices are crowded with people trying to find out "why" certain catastrophes, diseases, or relational breakdowns have occurred. Often our quest revolves around "who is to blame"—as few of us are willing to shoulder our full responsibility in the difficulties of life. Moreover, some things occur for which no one can be blamed or held fully responsible.

Sometimes our "why" questions border on the ridiculous. I read not too long ago of a rather humorous debate among insurance underwriters and clergy about whether or not a certain catastrophic event could be called an "act of God," that catch-all insurance term used for natural disaster. According to the story, lightning struck the venerable Yorkminster in York, England, and a great portion of the cathedral had burned. Would it not seem ludicrous to call that an "act of God," they questioned. The contention by some of the very conservative clergy that this event "must surely be the judgment of God on a liberal bishop" was hardly a sticking point for the insurance brokers!

Nevertheless, we humans always want to know "why." With the question "why" comes the possibility, we hope, of an answer that will give greater self-knowledge and potentially alter future behavior. As Aristotle, the great Greek philosopher and tutor of Alexander the Great, has taught many generations of seekers, our minds are so ordered that they cannot help trying to interpret the reality around them. On the first page of his *Metaphysics* he acknowledged the desire of all people "to know." We want to know who we are and how we fit in the world we inhabit.

In this sense, a person's true identity lies unfinished throughout all of life.[10] Being human is a dramatic, historical process. Our true self always lies ahead, to be fashioned with the tools of choice and action. The story is told about a young hiker coming upon a mountain cabin as he made his way along the Appalachian Trail. As he surveyed the whiskered old man rocking on the porch, he asked him, "Have you lived here all of your life?" The mountain man retorted, "Not yet!" We are becoming all of our lives. Living in time means change; some changes remain under our control, many do not.[11] Our potential or ideal self calls us beyond the present degree of self-expression into the possibility of becoming even more fully our true self. Thus, we are ever becoming human.

Several years ago I led a youth retreat for a church in Arkansas. I wanted to help those adolescents begin to explore potential vocations. One bright-eyed freshman boy could clearly articulate his goal to be a cardiologist. In response, I asked the clinker question: "But what will it take to get there?" With wisdom beyond his years and quiet confidence, he answered, "Patience and imagination"— a remarkable answer for a fourteen-year-old . . . or anyone.

Each of us has the gift of imagination that allows us to reflect on the distance between where we presently are and where we want to be.[12] Unfortunately, patience—which can allow a realistic approach to our dream—is what we more often lack. We have an added difficulty when our actions are ambiguous. Sometimes they seem to contradict what we imagine to be our true character. In such a case, we conclude that we have "betrayed" ourselves, suggesting that there is a certain continuity or essence to our identity. In the same way, when we notice that something is "out of character" for a person, we are assuming that this living human subject has a distinct pattern or form. But what determines one's "true self?"

All of us carry certain expectations concerning human behavior. These have been formed by various social influences, including family, church, and society. Because these influences and our appropriation of them varies, we must ask, "What, indeed, is acceptable human behavior?" In attempting to answer these difficult questions, we are faced with a major task of interpretation. In the search for our answers, though, we cannot go to a novel or historical essay and expect complete explication. Rather, our guide is found in the dynamic stories of humanity.

Decades ago, the father of the modern pastoral care movement, Anton Boisen, spoke of learning from "living human documents." This is precisely what we must do; the human person is only knowable in and through the process of living. We have a further important task, however, and that is to allow this mosaic of personal stories and cultural histories to give us a larger and more inclusive view of what it means to be human. To achieve this enlarged understanding of the mystery of our humanity, we will find it helpful to look closely at three contemporary ways of studying human beings.

Interpretations of Humanity

Studies of the human being such as sociology, psychology, and anthropology attempt to offer a precise description of what it means to be human. Often one of these scientific approaches takes on a rather pompous perspective, which assumes that it alone can   .

offer the proper interpretation. When that occurs, the particular science has moved from simply describing the human being to the much larger task of claiming to unlock the door to a comprehensive understanding. What might have begun as a more or less objective observation now presumes to dictate "how things ought to be." I can remember my surprise in a college psychology class to learn that Freud made the bold claim that his psychoanalytic method provided the key to knowing all about the human being. No single approach can make such a claim.

Three primary interpretations of human beings—biological, cultural, and religious—can help us understand our elusive nature. Each grows out of a particular comparison: humanity and the animals, humanity and other human beings, and humanity and the divine. As we examine these three perspectives, we should remember that while each sheds light, each is a partial view—which is hard for those of us utterly convinced of the superiority of our particular method of study. I remember a crusty seminary professor who had a stock line when his views were challenged: "Well, you don't have to agree with me; you have every right to be wrong!"

A Biological Interpretation

Biologically, we humans are uniquely different from any and all other forms of animal life that inhabit our planet.[13] One perceptive modern philosopher, Frederich Nietzsche, described the human as a "not yet fixed form of animal," meaning one who must consciously craft and adapt a way of life that can enable our survival. Because we are weak in instincts, we are not comfortably at home anywhere in the world without making adjustments. With no fur coat, turtle shell, or camel's hump to protect us, we are quite exposed to "the elements."

In a way that exceeds the other members of the animal world, however, our actions can show long-term purpose and planning. Through our ability to reflect on our needs and future, we can compensate for our physical limitations. We are well equipped for one of our primary tasks, that of constructing a habitable environment by means of technical ability and language.[14]

As a child growing up in northeastern Oklahoma, I never tired of hearing the stories of my great-grandparents traveling to Indian territory in covered wagons—complete with cows tied to the back. Traveling with stock and children was an arduous undertaking. Whether or not the Cherokee, Choctaw, and Creek tribes were really "civilized" was a daily concern. The goal of the Wiley family was to help evangelize these tribes, but they understood that cultivation of trusting relationships must precede the starting of churches. Furthermore, they knew they had to stick together in order to make a home in that rugged country.

This freedom of self-determination—the ability to choose—sets human beings apart from the instinctual responses of the animals.[15] The need to adapt has forced peoples over the centuries of time to develop sophisticated means of constructing a meaningful and rewarding lifestyle. In this sense, humanity shows its correspondence to the creator in that we share in the work of creation.

A true interpretation of humanity cannot be gained by examining the human being in abstract, for that is not how we live. We could not be humans without interaction with all of the aspects of the delicate web of life that comprises our environment.[16] Thus, the earth is truly our home. The joy of observing a child with a puppy or a practiced gardener delighting in the fragrance of his or her flowers reminds us that this world is more than simply a backdrop to our existence. Its harmony and beauty, tragedy and cataclysms are person-forming.

To a major extent, we are dependent upon all of the less complex life forms, for they are building blocks for our more developed lives.[17] Thus, we should offer them our protection and care.[18] The biological comparison of humanity with the animals can give partial insight into the distinctiveness of our lives, however. A comparison with other human beings will further our understanding of what it means to be human by illuminating further dimensions of our need for relationships.

A Cultural Interpretation

Cultural and social anthropologists are in agreement that we as human beings are social creatures. We do not just live; we live together. Humanity, from its earliest times, has lived in families, tribes, and ever more organized forms of social and political alliances.[19] One cannot be human in isolation. Individual human stories interlock; we are always political and social animals.

Living together, people inveterately create culture that expresses itself in social customs, communication, production, art, and history—just to name a few of its components. When we compare the different cultures within the one human family, we discover the unity of the great canvas of humanity, even though it stretches across enormous geographical distances. The common activities of human beings are organized into such divisions as tool-making, picture-language, and religious rituals.[20]

So we ask what we can learn about humanity by studying these patterns of association. First, we must notice a people's relationship to the land in which they live, for that will tell us much about their social identity. We are all rooted to a certain degree in this good earth. Hunting and gathering, as a means of making a living, are probably the most ancient forms of labor we know. These means are usually associated with the "Old Stone Age" or Paleolithic era.

The domestication of animals began at the same time as the growth of agriculture during the "New Stone Age" about 12,000 years ago. These same patterns still operate in many parts of our "post-modern" world. For example, Eskimo and Bedouin lifestyles continue to reflect this close affiliation with the land, although their nomadic populations are shrinking and the gentle methods of living in close relationship with their herds are becoming a thing of the past.

Second, we learn that human beings can be assisted as well as impoverished through their culture's level of technological development. The Industrial Revolution has allowed us progressively to shape and control, rather than merely respond to, our environments. Too often the reverence for the land and all living things associated with pastoral people is lost in the scramble for economic profit made possible by new inventions.

I recently visited Asheville, North Carolina, that lovely city nestled among the Smoky Mountains. As I drove toward Mount Mitchell one afternoon, I noticed the ranges of timber that were dying because of auto emission pollution. The sheer numbers of tourists, coupled with ineffective environmental control, were contributing to the gradual death of that magnificent area.[21]

Third, advanced technological achievements have contributed to a vast mobility for people all over the world. Even third world countries are becoming victims of urbanization. Changing family patterns accompany this wide-ranging human migration. One of my students, who is from Zimbabwe, where extended family relationships are much more carefully tended than here in America, has told me of the hardship this mobility imposes upon family ties. It is important both to bury and be buried among family members in their tribal land; otherwise, this foundational bond is dishonored and desecrated. Further, the scattering of families leads to strained marital and familial expectations. New divisions of labor between the sexes often accompany this new pattern that can be, for many, both disorienting and threatening. Many cultures are trying to juggle the increasing demand for childcare with the economic necessity for women to work outside the home.

Fourth, our contemporary awareness that the people of the earth must become a "global neighborhood" has, at the same time, led to a new emphasis on the "multi-cultural" nature of societies, neighborhoods, and workplaces. The American dream of a "melting pot," accented in an earlier day, now seems to be replaced by a rise in self-awareness for marginalized groups as well as new forms of ethnic friction. Understandably, people do not want their distinctiveness erased!

In New York City there has been a major refurbishing of Ellis Island, that reception center near the Statue of Liberty where more than 12,000,000 immigrants arrived in America in its peak years, 1892-1924. These persons of varying national backgrounds entered not only a new country but, in many respects, a new identity. The newly-opened Ellis Island museum seemingly stands more as a memorial to ideals of the past than a representation of the growing separatism of the complex present.

The very notion of an "American identity" is currently questioned. Many commentators speak, rather, of a "new tribalism." Different cultural expressions and economic development are both celebrated and feared. Racial antagonism is clearly seen in the resurgence of gang wars in the inner city. Unfortunately, crime and its punishment in our judicial system has more overtones of color now than at any time since the civil rights actions of the 1960s.

What will bind us together in a creative relationship? Will it be language, education, or a new culture forged out of the many patterned people that comprise our country? Will we become more like the builders of the Tower of Babel, confounded in language and purpose, or will we be persons working on a common quilt of hope and promise that can include our rich diversity as we look to the future? Do we have enough trust in one another to work for shared goals? What is it about being human that should call and enable us to build a hospitable community together?

A Religious Interpretation

Earlier we noted that expressions of human culture invariably include religious themes and rituals. Margaret Mead informed her readers several decades ago of the presence of religious activity in every culture she had investigated.[22] This universal inclination toward religious concern has been identified by some authorities as humanity's distinctive character. We exhibit a desire to worship. Irrespective of the nature of a people's cultural development, religion's powerful force has a key role in shaping human identity.[23] Shrines, holy days, and personal piety that sustain persons in their beliefs are the mortar that give many cultures their enduring stability.

While I do not believe that every religious expression is equally valuable, as many scholars of comparative religions argue, I do feel that the religious quest of humankind tells us something very important about people.[24] That we seek to give ourselves to something (someone) who can offer security and personal well being is a nearly universal phenomenon. So what does this teach us about the distinctiveness of humans?

Whenever I travel to a new city, especially abroad, I always visit the chief places of worship. After inspecting windows, icons, historical plaques, source of music, and pews, I can learn a great deal about the history and spirit of a particular people by observing the function these holy places serve in sustaining a surrounding village or metropolitan area. Of course, many of them no longer maintain a vibrant worshiping community. Their function is apparently more concerned now with the preservation of pristine architecture than with nourishing the lives of the faithful and the seekers. Often these houses of worship see only a trickle of folks coming for ongoing services. In the waning decade of the twentieth century, we can observe a growing secularism in many of the more economically developed nations. Traditional affirmations about God are being eclipsed.

As a theologian, people have asked me why, in a sophisticated, technologically advanced time, persons should be concerned with what seems to relate to a more primitive worldview. They may ask, "Isn't religion just an ideological tool to keep some people in the dark?" Throughout much of the twentieth century, Marxists have convinced many people that religion is no more than an "opiate" to keep the oppressed masses from pursuing economic justice through revolutionary means.

Others ask, "Doesn't religion depend upon myths or supposed historical events that no one can scientifically verify?" For many people, science has emerged in our time as the bearer of indisputable truth. They contend that if something can be measured, traced, or dissected, it can be granted status as a fact. Some people ask, "Doesn't religious devotion diminish the dignity and freedom of the person? After all, why should we need 'guidance' or 'sustenance' from some mysterious source beyond ourselves?" The French philosopher and writer Jean Paul Sartre asserted that any person who believed in God compromised his or her human freedom.[25]

Many persons flatly reject the idea that they have a need to worship. A young attorney remarked to me recently that he simply did not understand why people felt they needed to worship anything. "What does it add to one's life?" he asked. "Isn't it enough simply to be satisfied with one's profession and earning capacity?"

To his amazement, I suggested that possibly his profession and earning capabilities were the object of his worship. His workaholic drivenness made his protests about "how satisfied he was" a bit hard for me to swallow. Tragically, he seemed not to have the ability to probe his deeper self. His life was a constant succession of fitness clubs, the newest restaurants, shopping for just the right "power suit," and searching for new ways to impress his clients and senior partners with his professional stature. In reality he was lonely, discontented, and without a community of friendship and support. Increasingly, he faced difficulty in generating the motivation "to get ahead."

Long ago William Blake wrote, "Less than all cannot satisfy." My attorney friend surely wanted it all. He was simply not looking for the one who is All, God, the "Eternal Thou" who invites us to quench our deepest thirst through refreshing personal relationship. In his conversation with the woman of Samaria, Jesus described this sustaining presence of the spirit of God as "living water" (John 4:10).

I am convinced that all human beings long for a security that is stronger than we can create. Even though we buy insurance and try to save money, we know that we are defenseless against many things that can happen to us. We want to trust in God as the one who can give stability and purpose to this rapidly changing world. Who else can offer us ultimate security and hope?

The great Christian thinker, Augustine, confessed in his writings: "Thou hast made us for thyself, O God, and our hearts are restless until we rest in Thee." His years of searching led him to understand the futility of seeking happiness unrelated to the one who had created and sustained him all the days of his life. As with Augustine, we need to see that our restlessness is a sign of our true identity; we are not satisfied with "less than all."[26]

It is hard, however, for people today to discover much about their spiritual nature and need simply because our acquisitive society offers little to encourage us to pursue these inner concerns. Self-help remedies—be they psychological, physical, or motivational—often neglect our spiritual well-being. We are more than our physical urges and needs; our lives are bent toward our destiny created by God. Not only must we be in relationship with the natural world around us, including other humans, but we sigh to know more about our origins and future. We perceive that the mystery of our existence is wrapped up in the mystery of God. This other-oriented composition or nature may be the chief clue to the character of the mysterious human.

During my days as a student pastor in rural Kentucky, I learned a great deal of theology that I did not find in the books I was reading at school. My teacher was an elderly deacon who had spent his life working the soil, loving people, and being a faithful church member. Often he would lead in prayer in morning worship, and we knew to expect one phrase, in particular. He would always ask God to help us "remember where we came from," "how much we've got to do," and "how much we need one another to do it." I think his prayer offers a good summary of what it means to be human.

Endnotes

[1]Very helpful is the recent work of Brian McFague, *The Journey From Eden: Peopling Our World* (New York: Thames & Hudson, 1992).

[2]Most of us are unaware of the cultural ideologies that influence our lives. Indeed, the relationship between religion and culture may be the most difficult to recognize. See Jürgen Moltmann's discussion of religion and culture in Europe in *On Human Dignity*, trans. M. Douglas Meeks (Philadelphia: Fortress Press, 1984) 135ff.

[3]John MacQuarrie reminds us that Christianity has not always paid sufficient attention to humans as embodied with an inextricable relationship to the material world. This relationship, he argues, is best expressed by the word "having," with all the ambiguity it entails. See his extensive analysis in the work *In Search of Humanity* (New York: Crossroad, 1983) 72ff.

[4]George O. Kelsey, *Racism and the Christian Understanding of Man* (New York: Charles Scribner's Sons, 1965) 32, argues that the "logic of racism is genocide because what is wrong with an out-race is its fundamental being." A more contemporary, but brief, analysis of this same issue is provided by Cornel West in his book, *Prophecy Deliverance! An Afro-American Revolutionary Christianity* (Philadelphia: Westminster Press, 1982). The case could be made for the "feminization of poverty" as well. The marginization of women and children is well-documented. See Susan B. Thistlethwaite, *Sex, Race, and God: Christian Feminism in Black and White* (New York: Crossroad, 1989).

[5]Our spirituality expresses itself in asking questions of value. Clyde Crews charts this human activity in his theological primer, *Ultimate Questions* (New York: Paulist Press, 1986).

[6]See Margaret R. Miles, *Fullness of Life: Historical Foundations for a New Asceticism* (Philadelphia: Westminster, 1981).

[7]I am indebted to Stephen Crites' influential essay, "The Narrative Quality of Experience," *Journal of the American Academy of Religion*, 39 (September 1971) for this characterization. See also James William McClendon, Jr. *Biography as Theology: How Life Stories Can Remake Today's Theology* (Nashville: Abingdon, 1974).

[8]Norman Pittenger, *The Meaning of Being Human* (New York: Pilgrim Press, 1982) 6, suggests that perhaps the reason full self-understanding eludes us is because of the dynamic and unfinished nature of *becoming* a human being.

[9]Human suffering prompts the most wrenching inquiry. This is especially true for the person who affirms the goodness and power of God. Douglas John Hall, *God and Human Suffering* (Minneapolis: Augsburg, 1986) and Dorothee Sölle, *Suffering* (Philadelphia: Fortress, 1973) offer helpful treatments of the relationship of God to human suffering.

[10]P. Teilhard de Chardin, *The Future of Man* (London: Collins, 1964).

[11]Arthur C. McGill, *Death and Life* (Philadelphia: Fortress, 1987) 16-17, calls upon Americans to renounce their culture of optimism in order to live a more integrated life that acknowledges the reality of frustration, failure, and death.

[12]Basil M. Pennington, *Called: New Thinking on Christian Vocation* (New York: Seabury Press, 1983) reflects on the role imagination plays in vocational discernment. One must be able to imagine herself doing certain things in order to feel free to pursue the appropriate calling. See also Ray L. Hart, *Unfinished Man and the Imagination* (New York: Herder and Herder, 1968).

[13]Arnold Gehlen, *Man: His Nature and Place in the World*, trans. C. McMillan and K. Pillemer (New York: Columbia University Press, 1988) offers a comprehensive account of human reality from a biological perspective. See also Mary Midgley, *Beast and Man: The Roots of Human Nature* (Ithaca NY: Cornell University, 1978).

[14]Gehlen (40, 232, 336) points out that because of language, human reality transcends the specialization of most animal species and is world-open.

[15]Søren Kierkegaard reflects on the passion of subjectivity as the capacity to choose. See especially his *Concluding Unscientific Postscript*, trans. David Swenson (Princeton NJ: Princeton University Press, 1941).

[16]John and Mary Gribbin, *The One-Percent Advantage: The Sociobiology of Being Human* (Oxford: Blackwell, 1988) explores the biological roots of animal (and therefore also human) behavior.

[17]See Bernard G. Campbell, *Emerging Humankind*, 5th ed. (Los Angeles: University of California, 1988) 42-46.

[18]Douglas John Hall, *Imaging God: Dominion as Stewardship* (Grand Rapids MI: Eerdmans, 1986) calls Christians to learn to "be with" nature as God's caring presence.

[19]Hannah Arendt, *The Human Condition* (Chicago: University of Chicago Press, 1958) 46.

[20]For a general theory of social relations, see Gyorgy Lukacs, *The Ontology of Social Being*, trans. D. Fernbach (London: Merlin Press, 1978).

[21]I have been educated immensely by reading the national bestseller written by former Vice President Al Gore, *Earth in the Balance: Ecology and the Human Spirit* (New York: A Plume Book, 1992). For the theological warrant for ecological concern, see Sallie McFague's *Models of God: Theology for our Ecological, Nuclear Age* (Philadelphia: Fortress Press, 1987).

[22]Margaret Mead, *Continuities in Cultural Evolution* (New Haven CT: Yale University Press, 1964).

[23]Ninian Smart, *The Religious Experience of Mankind*, 2nd ed. (New York: Sheed and Ward, 1976).

[24]Wilfred Cantwell Smith, *The Meaning and End of Religion* (New York: Harper & Row, 1962, 1978).

[25]Sartre pursued the question of the meaningfulness of human life (without God, destiny, or purpose) through a variety of literary forms as in the novel *Nausea* (Norfolk CT: New Directions, 1949) and the play, *No Exit* (New York: A. A. Knopt, 1946).

[26]Abraham Joshua Heschel, *I Asked for Wonder* (New York: Crossroad, 1988) 38, characterizes the root of religion as "the question what to do with the feeling for the mystery of living, what to do with awe, wonder, and amazement."

The Creation of Humanity

As we have noted in our exploration of what it means to be human, people are always asking questions. "Where do babies come from?" is usually asked before anyone is quite prepared to answer. At such moments the mother and father groan inwardly, thinking, "I thought I had a few more years before I had to answer this!"

People have been asking this question in some form or fashion from the beginning of time. Where did we come from? Were we planned by a benevolent creator, or are we simply a fortunate product of a long, drawn-out cosmic process? Why are we here? Where are we going? Are we able to choose our destiny? Why do persons look so different in appearance yet have so much in common?

The human person poses a mystery: we are creatures, while at the same time we are unquestionably different from all other creatures. According to the psalmist, we are paradoxical beings, "a little lower than God and crowned with glory and honor" (Ps 8).[1] Dustiness and dignity are wrapped together in our humanity.

In their mythology, the Greeks used the figure of the centaur to picture the mixed character of the human being. This colorful mythological half-horse and half-human—the human torso swept upward toward the heavens with its animal legs firmly planted on the earth—seemed to capture the ambiguity of human lives. We realize our finitude and creaturely needs, yet we long to be set free from these constraints and soar upward like the divine.

Most of us know something of the ambivalence that our unique identity presents. While we as human beings share much with other animal forms—the struggle for survival, a limited temporal horizon, and assorted physical needs, to mention the most obvious—we are more than biologically determined.[2] The capacity to question our personal existence and special relationship to God sets us apart from other creatures.[3] Therefore, we can never be content living at subhuman level; something within each of us stretches out for more.

I recall a visit to the Metropolitan Museum of Art in New York City. As I walked through that majestic and cavernous structure, I marveled again at the human spirit's desire to interpret the world, especially our place within it. Statuaries, tapestries, musical instruments, and early maps all bear witness to the human quest to understand our beginnings and destiny. These interpretive expressions reveal the unique status of the human person and vividly portray a great curiosity about our relationship to the natural world and possible supernatural origins.

God the Creator

Every culture has its own version of the creation story.[4] Whether described as a great cosmic battle that causes the division of night and day, or the defeat of a great sea monster that allows the sea and land to coexist peacefully, or the prolific reproduction of the gods or goddesses that results in the inhabited world, each story attempts to establish a foundation for our present existence.

To be sure, our modern attempts to picture the beginning of things take on a more sophisticated shape. In our attempt to understand our origin as humans, we hope to unlock some of the mystery of our personhood. The various sciences have studied specific dimensions of our humanity, for example, through the study of specific patterns such as linguistics, tool-making, or geographical migration.[5] Each such attempt has demonstrated that no one approach is adequate, however. This leads us to admit that the human person cannot be fully explained or understood by any observable scientific method. In addition to these studies, our distinctiveness as human beings requires a theological interpretation. A study of the origin of humanity that includes this dimension can give us significant direction in our understanding of the meaningfulness of our lives.

A theological understanding interprets our beginnings as a creation of God. This particular understanding becomes clear through the biblical texts, the progressive thinking and insights of Christians across the centuries, dialogue with the findings of the human and natural sciences, and a balanced use of reason. Our task today is to draw these materials together into a comprehensive interpretation.

Theology is the study of God, and it insists that God is knowable because God wants to be known, as much as finite humans can know of the infinite. Of course, we can never really know and understand the mystery of God. Saint Augustine was correct when he said, "If you have understood, then what you have understood is not God." Yet, we should confront the reality of God as creator and sustainer of creation and human persons as having been created in God's image. Indeed, we must examine God and the human person together to understand the intended intimacy of our relationship.

This calls for us to employ a "faith that seeks understanding," by paying attention not only to our present context, but to the history that lies behind our faith, which requires us to use our sources with great care. As you remember, on the first day of class, most teachers inform the students of both the nature of the course and the means or methodology by which best to understand the new material. I recall that in my first chemistry lab, the professor sought to dispel any notion of blowing up the building or turning all the sophomore students green. He patiently explained how we would conduct our experiments and then write our results in a lab book. He also made it clear that if we failed to follow proper procedures, our information would not be valid. Shortcuts were banned!

One year two American organ transplant pioneers won the coveted Nobel prize in medicine. When interviewed about the award, one of the physicians noted the importance of clearly defining "what question is being asked, is it being asked properly, and will it give us an answer." Through careful research, these doctors had refined the procedure for transplanting bone marrow from one person to another, which resulted in prolonging the life of many people.

We need to be as thorough as the doctors when we inquire about human origins. The best place to begin our search is with an examination of the biblical material. Here in story form, ancient writers gave us a foundation for making sense of our lives.

Biblical Perspective

Biblical statements are essentially theological in nature. Rather than instructing us in biology, astronomy, or geology, the biblical writers gave us confessions of faith, spoken from experience and inspiration. They were preoccupied with why we are here, not how or when. The chief concern of the Bible is to speak of our relationship to God; indeed, its writers could find no way to describe humanity except in such relational terms.[6]

The Bible has been described as filled with models of the ways in which we relate to God—both proper and improper ways of relating. The Bible does not present a fully developed interpretation of what it means to be human, yet it does offer an interpretive key to understanding humanity by reflecting on the beginnings of humanity.[7]

The Genesis writers were not writing a scientific account or history as such. Rather they were trying to make sense of that early epoch of human existence that lay behind their covenantal history with Yahweh, those years before Abraham and Sarah.

The Genesis narratives tell us that God spoke, and the world was created out of nothing! We do not know when or how this took place. From our understanding, creation from nothing is completely incomprehensible.[8] Consequently, we will do well to accept as trustworthy the Bible's explanation. God willed it, and creation became a reality because of the divine spoken word. The writer of Hebrews expressed it well,

> By faith we understand that the worlds were prepared by the word of God, so that what is seen was made from things that are not visible. (11:3)

This Bible passage does not mean that a fully complete world emerged in six twenty-four-hour days, but a process began that fulfilled God's purpose and provided hospitable conditions for the emergence of varied forms of life.[9] (I am always careful to assure my nephews that just because the text does not specifically mention the dinosaurs does not mean they never existed).

Then according to the biblical narrative, when God's initial work of creation was completed, "God saw everything that he had made, and indeed, it was very good" (Gen 1:31). While God called it good, even very good, it was not yet finished. God can be likened to a great composer who begins with a simple melody and improvises toward a harmonious, interlocking fugue. Creation continues.

That God is the creator of the human race is a central biblical conviction. Further, we as human beings are an intentional, unique, and special creation. Two complementary accounts of God's creation of human beings are found in the Book of Genesis, each with particular emphases and insights.

Genesis 1–2:4 is a liturgical text, celebrating in the form of a hymn God's deliberate actions in bringing forth creation. The structure of this passage shows the movement from less developed to more complex forms of life. Upon our human family God invokes a special blessing and assigns to us a unique job description: to fill the earth and care for it. Other living things will be dependent upon us as caretakers of God's creation.[10]

Our dignity as humans rests upon our origin, from God, and our vocation as the leaders of all the creatures. The Genesis passage assumes that God is the source of all that is, the true God, who will later be revealed to the people of covenant.[11] Not only does our human family bear a special likeness to God, but our vocation entails a partnership with the Creator.

Genesis 2:5-25 offers a different, more descriptive account of the creation of humans. It begins with a portrait of the garden God prepared as a home for our ancestors and stresses our connection as human beings to it. The Hebrew writers used a pun to link humankind and the earth by contrasting two very similar words, *adam* (humanity) and *adamah* (the ground). Thus, we as humans are earthy, dusty creatures, grounded in the soil we must till and to which we must return.

The beautiful picture of God stooping in the mud to form the human persons, sharing with these special beings the very breath of life, God's own spirit, suggests the intimacy of God's relationship to these unique creatures. One of my bright students solved the age-old question about whether or not Adam and Eve had navels by suggesting "God had poked them in the middle while they were still damp." I do believe there are more significant insights to be gleaned from this text!

This text gives a clue as to the composition of human beings. Often we hear persons described as made up of "body and soul" or "body, soul, and spirit." Scripture does speak of the human in this way, but quite sparingly. It is much more concerned to stress that humans are unified beings; therefore, we cannot be cleanly divided into these components.[12] A person's body is inseparable from that person's very self. The text "and the man [human] became a living being" (Gen 2:7) simply means that this one is a living creature, an organic whole animated by God's creative act— "lively clay," as one of my teachers liked to say.

The Greeks spoke of the body as "the prison house of the soul," as if the human body was evil while the soul was good, even divine.[13] The Bible, however, accentuates the goodness of the body as the means of personal self-expression in the world and never speaks of the soul in a disembodied sense. Our bodies place us in solidarity with all other persons and make possible our relating to them.[14] The Hebrew scriptures speak of a person's relatives as one's "flesh" (Gen 37:27) or one's "bone and flesh" (Gen 2:23). The New Testament also stresses our wholeness and the kinship we enjoy with all human beings.

While the Bible uses the language of the human "soul" to denote a special relationship to God, it never suggests that the soul is a "divine spark," as in the Platonic tradition. We as humans are not divine, but are created to live in obedience and friendship to God. This ancient account in Genesis 2 also accents the inter-dependence of the sexes and a simplicity of life close to nature. In naming the animals, Adam demonstrated superiority to them and human care for these other creatures. God informed our forebears of the limits that they as humans had to respect, or dire conse-quences would occur. God is identified as Yahweh, the God of Israel, who revealed the holy name to Moses.

The Bible also affirms that God is the creator of each human being. The Protestant reformer, Martin Luther, said that if one really believes in God as the creator of the world, then one is obliged to confess: "God created me." We know that we did not create ourselves nor simply inherit our distinctive personalities. I remember my folks shaking their heads trying to figure out which side of the family was responsible for my mischief; there was no consensus, as you might imagine.

Varied biblical texts speak of God's "knowing" an individual even before birth. A most graphic portrayal of God's intimate intention for a unique person is found in Jeremiah's testimony: "Before I formed you in the womb I knew you, and before you were born I consecrated you; I appointed you a prophet to the nations" (Jer 1:5). The psalmist also confessed "It was you who formed my inward parts; you knit me together in my mother's womb" (Ps 139:13). These texts inform us of God's personal interest in and intimate knowing of all dimensions of our lives. Indeed, our creaturely existence is purposeful.

God did not just start the process of human procreation, but is dynamically involved in the whole human process. As persons of faith, we realize that in one and the same event we were both created by God and given life by our mothers and fathers. Even small children know that mom and dad do not really go to the hospital to pick up a baby (presumably delivered by the stork, God's beaked messenger), but to deliver "what has been growing in mommy's tummy." Christian families gratefully receive the newborn as indeed a gift from God, but they are aware that their cooperation was needed.

The old catechisms of the church speak not only of God as the creator, but also as the sustainer of creation.[15] The one who set in motion the wonder of our world has not ceased to work creatively toward the divine intention. This is particularly evident in God's willingness to bring creation to its intended destiny through redemption in Christ. Thus, we are not deists who believe that God simply wound up the world like a great clock and let it run on its own. Rather, we believe that the world and the humans in it have a relative freedom; yet we are not abandoned to fend for ourselves. God as the creative, brooding Spirit continues to move in the world, making possible new life.[16]

The New Testament adds a significant insight to the Old Testament's teaching about creation. It tells us that the agent of creation was the Word of God. The prologue to the fourth gospel offers this perspective: "All things came into being through him, and without him not one thing came into being" (John 1:3). From the very beginning, the world was created to bear the stamp of the one who "became flesh and lived among us, full of grace and truth" (John 1:14).[17]

The apostle Paul added a similar understanding through the use of an early Christian hymn that celebrates the role that the son of God plays in creation. The hymn describes Christ as "the image of the invisible God" and acknowledges that "all things were created through him and for him" (Col 1:16).[18] When we understand that we were created to bear the likeness of the human expression of our God, we realize that we are "crowned with glory and honor."

A Contemporary Scientific Interpretation

Our biblical understanding and the picture of the world offered to us by modern science are not easy to join together. I think part of the difficulty comes from holding false expectations of these separate but complementary ways of knowing truth. For instance, one contemporary approach to the question of "where did we come from?" called "Scientific Creationism"[19] attempts to prove certain views of the origin of humanity, as well as the age of the earth and the reality of the flood, by using the biblical materials as scientific evidence. While the biblical materials reflected the ancient cosmogonies and must certainly today be in dialogue with science, they were not written as scientific accounts. Thus, we must not use the biblical narratives in a way that they were never intended to be used.

Science and theology are really asking different questions. Science inquires about how something occurs, and theology asks about the why and the who. Thus, conflict between the Bible and science is unnecessary.[20] Conflict arises when scientists stray from their proper field and start making theological or anti-theological assertions, or when theologians condemn scientific investigation as undermining the teaching of the Bible. Obviously, we should find a way to combine a theological understanding of the creation of human beings with the best insights of current scientific research.

The basic consensus among biologists about human beginnings is some form of emergent evolution. Just how evolution works is the subject of much discussion among today's biologists.[21]

One idea is that evolution is gradually occurring at all times because of mutations and changing environmental influences.[22] Another proposal is that long periods of relative evolutionary stability are punctuated by sudden appearances of new species, which is called punctuated equilibrium.[23] Scientists theorize that perhaps both processes are in operation. Evolutionary theories about the origins of humanity can be quite compatible, I believe, with the Christian view of creation and maintain a high regard for biblical authority.

During graduate school I became acquainted with a student who had grown up in Kenya, the son of missionaries. While still an adolescent, he began studying the fascinating research of the paleontologists and anthropologists concerning human origins. This pursuit provoked a crisis of faith for him. How could he reconcile these findings with the dominant theological tradition of his church? He wrestled with these questions during his years of premed studies and found them growing more persistent. Finally, my friend realized that he could have no peace until he found a way to reconcile his belief in God as loving creator with the long history of struggle that antedates and characterizes the history of the human being. So he entered seminary to pursue theological studies. His graduate thesis explored the possibility that "natural selection" was God's intended means of propagating the species. He found a way to combine his faith in God as creator with the science in which he had been schooled since his primary years. This discovery brought him great joy and the encouragement to pursue ministry as a vocation.

To suggest that God uses the evolutionary process as the means of creative activity does not lessen God's purpose or presence. Some persons maintain that it qualifies divine power to speak of a lengthy process of development. Somehow God seems more powerful to them if creation occurs instantaneously, that is, by divine fiat. I prefer to think of God continually bringing forth new possibilities within creation through the ever present Holy Spirit because of the intimacy of relationship such a model suggests. Of course, we cannot simply identify God with the creative processes of the world, but neither can we conclude that God is ever absent from them.[24]

We must not fear dialogue with science in the shared quest for truth, even though difficulties may occur. For instance, just as it is difficult to say when a child becomes accountable for his or her actions, it is also difficult to say exactly when our forebears became *Homo sapiens*, which literally means "one that knows." Most scientists assume that as humans evolved from lower forms of life, the result was groupings of the new species. We cannot prove biologically, however, if there was a literal "first pair" or numerous scattered groupings of persons. In my mind, the truth of the biblical account is not dependent upon resolving this question.[25] At the risk of sounding like an article right out of *National Geographic*, let me give a simplified overview of current scientific understanding about our origin as human beings.

Africa, the birthplace of the earliest biped, has also been a home to all subsequent species. Modern anthropologists such as Louis B. Leakey believe that the line of hominids leading to human beings diverged from the apes at least 20,000,000 years ago. Four australopithecines (a small-brained ancestor of the human) have been found only in Africa, as was *Homo habilis* (a hominid with greater dexterity and skill).

Equipped with a larger brain and specialized stone tools, the sole successor, *Homo erectus*, moved beyond Africa, reaching Java, China, and probably southern Europe. Contemporary scientific studies date our *Homo erectus* ancestors from about 1.6 million years to 300,000 years ago. The earliest most distinguishing characteristic of these "distant cousins" was not a large brain, language, or tool-making, but the ability to walk upright. "Uncle Ugh" (as my teacher Dale Moody liked to call one of these early forebears) was a pretty likable chap. His visitors could count on a good meal of fresh meat and a warm fire in the entrance to the cave when spending the night. Only *Homo sapiens* spread farther, populating northern Europe and Siberia and, perhaps by 50,000 years ago, moving on to Australia by sea and later walking across the Bering Strait to the Western Hemisphere.

The vast sweep of human history can boggle our minds, but reassurance comes from remembering that God stands behind the process and works creatively within it.

An Integration of Faith and Science

A comprehensive understanding of our human beginnings must combine theological as well as scientific insights, as we have seen. As complementary truths, they provide a significant portrait of this unique member of creation. Indeed, through integrating their respective insights, we can see that the paradoxical identity of human beings can only be understood through exploring our relationship to the natural world[26] as well as to that which is transcendent, the living God.

One of the reasons for the church's opposition to theories of evolution is the commonality suggested between animals and human beings. This bond really should not disturb us; it could serve to remind us of our uniqueness in comparison. Anyone who has ever visited the ape house at a zoo can usually recognize a relative among them! Patterns of grooming, infant care, turf protection—all look amazingly familiar to those with only a slight imagination.

Our commonality with these entertaining, yet intelligent anthropoids should not be a cause for shame, but for wonder at the amazing process by which the self-conscious mind emerged. We owe these creatures much for our own, more developed patterns of living. By God's richly complex intent, our common ancestors have contributed significant qualities to our continued existence. Indeed, we are dependent upon all forms of life that have preceded us.[27]

Many ecclesiastical leaders and laypersons have contended that if one accepts an evolutionary view of the species, that somehow the human as a unique creation of God will be sacrificed.

Persons of this persuasion would do well to read again the early chapters of Genesis in which the common origin and relationship between the animals and human beings is readily acknowledged. After the aquatic animals and the birds were created on the fifth day, the land animals and persons were made together on the last day of creation (Gen 1:24f). According to the creation account found in Genesis 2, Adam was in the company of the animals until he became aware that his need for companionship was not satisfied.

Elsewhere in the Old Testament, the common lot of people and animals is strongly emphasized—while fully recognizing the difference. When God preserved Noah and his family through the flood, the ark was filled with "two of every kind," as well as extra "clean animals" for them to eat. The Bible simply assumes that we cannot be human without recognizing that our lives are bound up with all of God's creatures.[28]

Most importantly, the New Testament affirms that the redemption of the human being has implications for all of creation. Creation, too, will experience the liberty of the sons and daughters of God (Rom 8:23f). For these reasons the Christian church should acknowledge as part of God's plan the basic connection of animals and human persons. I must admit, however, nineteenth-century England would have missed some colorful preaching if the church had been less vehement in its response to the discoveries of biology.

Regarding the human as a unique creation of God does not depend upon full-grown humans appearing at God's spoken word or God literally forming persons out of dust. It has more to do with knowing our true character, "made in the image of God."

The rabbis have a saying: "To know where you are going, you must know where you have come from." The creation of humanity tells us much about our destiny. That you and I have minds with which to question our existence lets us know that we are created for a significant purpose and have a God-given responsibility to discover and pursue it. We also have the ability to know that we are more than accidents in the evolutionary process.[29] A reflective mind in the human certainly suggests that we are not simply the product of impersonal forces, but the good creation of the Eternal Thou, who is the truly knowing one.

Our personhood corresponds to our creator, who is truly personal, which means we will become who we are created to be by attending to this primary relationship. Just as the world can only be properly understood when it is seen as a creation of God, so it is with human beings. Our origin tells us our destiny. God gives to us as human beings our foundational unity: a common creator an equality of dignity, a divinely intended destiny.

In the novel by Olive Ann Burns, *Cold Sassy Tree*, Grandpa Blakeslee instructs young Will Tweedy, his grandson, about the goodness of life given by God.

> Faith ain't no magic wand or money-back gar'ntee, either one. Hit's jest a way a-livin'. Hit means you don't worry th'ew the days. Hit means you go'n be holdin' on to God in good or bad times, and you accept whatever happens. Hit means you respect life like it is—like God made it.[30]

Hardly eloquent, but Grandpa's words brim with understanding.

Our lives have meaning because we are God's creation, with a particular vocation to care for all of creation. Life can be filled with purpose and hope for us because our lives come from God and we can spend our lives fulfilling our calling as God's thinking, adaptable, and responsive creatures. It is good that we can question what it means to be human, for that is the best way to gain new insights about our dignity and destiny.

As we know, a child can receive no more damaging message than that he or she is not wanted. Children who constantly hear "how much trouble they are to raise," "how good life would be without them," and "when will you ever grow up?" are not likely to believe that they matter very much. As human beings, the Bible tells us that we matter greatly to God, so much that God desires to share life with us as our creator and companion. When we understand our beginnings and purpose, our lives take on the God-given significance that is meant to be ours.

Endnotes

[1]Arthur Weiser, *The Psalms*, trans. Herbert Hartwell, Old Testament Library (Philadelphia: Westminster Press, 1962) 142, reminds us that the revelation of God and human self-awareness are intimately bound up with each other.

[2]Wolfhart Pannenberg, *Anthropology in Theological Perspective*, trans. Matthew J. O'Connell (Philadelphia: Westminster Press, 1985) 22, contends that human biology has a limited role in constructing a theological anthropology because the "question it asks about the human being is undoubtedly fundamental, but it is not comprehensive."

[3]Karl Rahner, *Foundations of Christian Faith*, trans. William V. Dych (New York: Crossroad, 1978) describes this capacity as "transcendental experience," which means that humans are always oriented toward the holy mystery.

[4]Langdon Gilkey, *Maker of Heaven and Earth* (Garden City NY: Anchor Books, 1959) 45-47.

[5]E.g., Hannah Arendt, *The Human Condition* (Chicago: University of Chicago Press, 1958) and Gyorgy Lukacs, *The Ontology of Social Being*, trans. D. Fernbach (London: Merlin Press, 1978).

[6]Douglas John Hall describes this approach to humanity as an "ontology of communion," specifically, being with God and being with humankind. See his very helpful study *Imaging God: Dominion as Stewardship* (Grand Rapids MI: Eerdmans, 1986). See also Carter Heyward, *The Redemption of God: A Theology of Mutual Relation* (Lanham MD: University Press of America, 1982) for another perspective on the primacy of relation.

[7]For a comprehensive review of the Genesis narratives on the creation of humanity, see Edmund Hill, *Being Human* (London: Geoffrey Chapman, 1984) and Phyllis Trible, *God and the Rhetoric of Sexuality* (Philadelphia: Fortress Press, 1978).

[8]Gilkey, 52, stresses that the formula *creatio ex nihilo* basically means "Creation is the divine evocation into existence, out of nothingness, of finite being in its totality."

[9]I have been helped greatly by Arthur Peacocke's Bampton Lectures of 1978, published as *Creation and the World of Science* (Oxford: Clarendon Press, 1979), which interfaces current scientific theory of cosmic origination with an understanding of humanity as God's creation.

[10]That we have failed in this dimension of our humanity is noted by Bill McKibben's dramatic lament, *The End of Nature* (New York: Random House, 1989). See also Sallie McFague, *The Body of God: An Ecological Theology* (Minneapolis: Fortress Press, 1993) for a sustained theological reflection on our proper place in the world.

[11]Indeed, reflection by Israel upon its experience of the Exodus led to a theology of creation. Thus, belief in God as creator and redeemer are inseparable in the Hebrew scriptures. See the helpful analysis of Paul K. Jewett, *God Creation, and Revelation* (Grand Rapids Ml: Eerdmans, 1991) 460ff, and G. Von Rad, *Old Testament Theology* (New York: Harper, 1962) 136ff.

[12]Hans Walter Wolff, *Anthropology of the Old Testament* (Philadelphia: Fortress Press, 1974) 7.

[13]See Plato's *Republic*, Books 4-6, and *The Laws*, as well as the Stoic writings of Marcus Aurelius.

[14]Erving Goffman examines the social sphere of interpersonal relations in *Encounters: Two Studies in the Sociology of Interaction* (Indianapolis: Bobbs-Merrill, 1961). Although the research is dated, the insights remain relevant.

[15]This implies an understanding of continuous creation rather than maintaining the "original paradoxical condition of creation," according to Jürgen Moltmann, *God in Creation* (San Francisco: Harper & Row, 1985) 208.

[16]Arthur Peacocke reminds us that "we have to identify God's actions within the processes themselves . . . and this identification means we must stress more than ever before God's *immanence* in the world," *God and the New Biology* (San Francisco: Harper & Row, 1986) 95.

[17]John A. T. Robinson, *The Human Face of God* (Philadelphia: Westminster Press, 1973) 154, is persuaded that "Christ is seen throughout the New Testament as the expression and agent of God's purpose from the start."

[18]Actually the apostle has probably reworked a pre-Pauline hymn to accent further the cosmic and reconciling work of the redeemer, according to Ralph Martin, *Ephesians, Colossians, and Philemon*, Interpretation (Atlanta: John Knox Press, 1991) 104-105.

[19]E.g., Thomas F. Heinze, *Creation vs. Evolution*, 2nd rev. ed. (Grand Rapids MI: Baker Book House, 1973).

[20]Eric Rust, revered professor of Christian philosophy at Southern Baptist Theological Seminary, demonstrated this complementarity in his classic work *Science and Faith: Toward a Theological Understanding of Nature* (New York: Oxford University Press, 1967).

[21]J. Z Young, *An Introduction to the Study of Man* (Oxford: Clarendon Press, 1971) offers a comprehensive discussion.

[22]Jeffrey S. Wicken, *Evolution, Thermodynamics and Information: Extending the Darwinian Program* (New York: Oxford University Press, 1987).

[23]Peacocke, 53.

[24]This point is made profoundly by Pedro Trigo: "Creation implies a universal activity in the world on the part of God, and a total referral of that world to God." See Trigo's *Creation and History* (Maryknoll NY: Orbis, 1991) 98.

[25]Ted Peters, ed. *Cosmos as Creation: Theology and Science in Consonance* (Nashville-Abingdon Press, 1989) 13-14. See also John Polkinghorne, *One World: The Interaction of Science and Theology* (Princeton: Princeton University Press, 1986).

[26]H. Paul Santmire, *The Travail of Nature: The Ambiguous Ecological Promise of Christian Theology* (Philadelphia: Fortress Press, 1980) offers a review of the theology of nature in both testaments of the Bible.

[27]See John Carmody, *Ecology and Religion: Toward a New Christian Theology of Nature* (New York: Paulist Press, 1983), especially Chapter 8.

[28]Jürgen Moltmann records: "The right of human beings to rule over the non-human creation must therefore be balanced by their respecting the 'rights' of the nonhuman creation," *On Human Dignity: Political Theology and Ethics* trans. M. Douglas Meeks (Philadelphia: Fortress Press, 1984) 27.

[29]A helpful treatment comes from Philip Hefner, "The Evolution of the Created Co-Creator," in Peters, 211-34.

[30]Olive Ann Burns, *Cold Sassy Tree* (Boston: G. K. Hall & Co., 1985) 563.

The Dignity of Humanity

Human beings are multifaceted, unique creations of God. Part of our distinctive identity (and responsibility!) is the ability to ask questions about our world and, particularly, about ourselves. Asking questions of value is an index of our spirituality. In this chapter, we will attempt to answer the question, "What does the Bible mean when it speaks of 'the image of God'?" The answer to this question can offer a central clue to what it means for a person to become fully human.

Biblical Perspectives on the Image of God

The first chapter of the Bible tells us something very important about human beings: we are created "in the image and likeness of God" (Gen 1:26-27). Humans were not made "according to their kind" like the other creatures, but for a special caring relationship to God, other humans, and all of creation—which is the meaning of "the image of God".[1] This description tells us a great deal about our status—"a little lower than the angels"—and our calling.

How important to reclaim this central truth about our true identity in a day when human life seems to be of so little value! Headlines blare the tragedy of children caught in the neighborhood crossfire of drug merchants. If persons view themselves with so little significance that they will waste their lives for the momentary high of cocaine, it is not surprising that they have negligible regard for others.

In every age, students of the Bible have tried to determine exactly what the writer of Genesis meant by the unparalleled characterization of women and men as in the image of God.[2] Remarkably, this concept is not developed elsewhere in the Old Testament, with the exception of a brief mention in Genesis 5:1 and 9:6. In the first passage, the writer notes that humans still bear the image of God, even though the sin of eating from the forbidden tree had already occurred. (We will explore the meaning of "fallen" in the next chapter). The second passage notes that after the Flood, God made a covenant with humans. One feature of this agreement between God and Noah's family (representing all human beings) was that no human should take the life of another, because each is "in the image of God" (Gen 9:6).

The two words "image and likeness" reappear together however, in Exodus 20:4:

> You shall not make for yourself an idol, whether in the form of
> anything that is in heaven above, or that is in the earth beneath,
> or that is in the water under the earth.

I have discovered that if we examine these passages together we can glean a better sense of the meaning of "image of God."

This verse in Exodus, the second of the Ten Commandments, clearly stands as a warning against idolatry. Surrounded by other cultures with competing views about God (or often, many gods), the writers of the Hebrew scriptures were always concerned to declare that the God of Israel, Yahweh, was the true and living God. Yahweh had made a covenant with Israel, thereby convincing the people that their neighbors were following false gods, often represented by "graven images" set up in their places of worship. The Babylonians, for example, finished constructing a temple for worship by placing an idol of their god in its sanctuary.

The word our Bible uses for "image" is the same Hebrew word for "idol." The law forbids persons to make idols to represent the divine. How could one love and serve what was the creation of his or her own hands? When the Israelites insisted on making the "golden calf" in the wilderness as a substitute god, they displayed the depth of their rebellion against the living God, as the account in Exodus 32 tells us.

The writer of Genesis 1 was aware that no "graven image" could adequately represent God and that to fashion such was idolatry. Indeed, he or she may have had the Babylonian ritual in mind when inspired to write this overture to the first testament. Thus, as the conclusion of this hymn of praise about creation, the writer describes humans as "the image and likeness of God." Rather than needing to create an idol for worship, like their Babylonian neighbors, they were to realize that God had created them to bear God's image and likeness on the earth. This did not mean that they were to worship the creature rather than the creator, but that they had a special, God-given responsibility on the earth.[3]

Of all the creatures God made, only humanity could hear the address of God and respond.[4] At some point in the long process of evolution, our forebears crossed the line of demarcation where they became human. They were able, then, to stand in a relationship to the creator in which they could correspond as responsible partners. This comprises what we describe as being "created in the image of God."

Being in the image of God does not mean our ability to walk upright or our ability to reason, as some earlier interpreters imagined. It means being gifted with the capacity to relate meaningfully to God and others. Humanity was called from nothing into being through the creative word of God. The goal of that lengthy development was the capacity to respond freely in love to the creative one who calls. We are able to hear the beckoning, quiet address of our creator through the beauty of the world, the words of scripture, and the voices of other humans.

Bearing the image of God must imply that humanity is created to speak—like God can speak—and is uniquely equipped to perceive and respond to the creative word as well as to speak it as God's representative. Words fashion our relationships, just as God's word makes possible any relating at all.

Have you ever observed the emergence of language in a child? This little one can now order the world around her or him in descriptive, often demanding ways. The newly-found ability to identify his or her surroundings and significant others gives rise to all sorts of creative endeavors.

I spent a weekend in the home of two of my former students, whom I had the privilege of uniting in marriage. Two daughters, ages four and two, kept this family quite busy. The younger girl was just learning the power of words, and she tried them out with abandon. Her speech enabled her to interpret what she was experiencing without resorting to wails of discomfort or glee or tossing grapes on the floor. She was beginning to understand certain words, and I knew that a conversation with her was just around the corner. She will remember those words that will best suit her two-year-old purposes.

Human speech allows a dimension of communion unique to our identity and vocation. Conversations shape our identity. All of a person's life is a response to God—either a yes or a no. As the reformer Martin Luther never tired of reminding his hearers and readers, we cannot escape God. Every aspect of our lives is lived *coram deo*, or in the presence of God.[5]

Somehow the idea that God knows all about us, even better than we know ourselves, gets lost as we mature. I remember as a child having the distinct sense that nothing was hidden from God. In a Dennis the Menace cartoon, Dennis is having a conversation with his pal, Joey, who is about to engage in some mischief. Knowingly, Dennis offers this warning: "I would be careful, Joey; God writes down everything we do and then reports it to Santa." We might quibble with his theology, but his instincts were correct, at least about God! God is probably not making a list in preparation for Christmas, but surely is aware of all aspects of our lives and wants to relate to us in them.

Humans Serving Creation

Not only does God call humans into being, God also calls the human family into special service on behalf of creation. The special task entailed in bearing God's image in creation is spelled out in Genesis 1:26-30 and Genesis 2:15-20. Humans are to have "dominion" over all living things, all other animals as well as the trees and plants. Dominion includes care, an aspect too often neglected by modernity's rapacious appetite.[6]

In naming the animals, the human demonstrates the calling to serve as God's representative to care for God's creation. Naming God's creatures[7] is a way of recognizing the unique significance each has within creation. It is a way of establishing a relationship; hence, the Old Testament places much importance upon the power of naming.

Saint Augustine was especially fond of the narrative (Gen 2:19-20) about the origin of the animals' names. To him, finding names for the great variety of animals was evidence of Adam's intellectual prowess! Whatever prompted one to think of hippopotamus, duck-billed platypus, or hyena, anyway?!

We are called to be co-creators and co-workers with God on earth. Francis of Assisi can be our teacher in this. He believed that the world was the *form* in which God may be known, loved, and served. Thus he labored as a peacemaker among all creatures great and small.

Only the human, among God's creatures, can take due account of the needs of humans and of nature; hence, we are given the task of caring for all creatures and their environment. In my judgment, one of the best ways a child can learn to treasure God's creation is to bear primary responsibility (when old enough) for a beloved pet. This can teach the child on a daily basis how dependent creation is upon the care of those called to "tend the garden."

Adults also need to be taught by pets of the joy present in relating lovingly to God's creatures.

If you have not guessed it already by the last two paragraphs, yes, I do have an "animal companion," as the politically correct would say. His name is Martin Luther Marshall-Green, which honors the German and theological heritage of this lively Schnauzer. We obtained him about six years ago when he was eleven months old; his former mistress said she was "too old to cook for him." We soon discovered that her words meant that no Gravy Train had ever touched his lips! Our first task was to let him know of the goodness of being a dog, his unique calling in life.

Luther reminds me that all of creation reflects God's generous heart and creative delight and that we are to forge a "peaceable kingdom" whenever possible. Luther also serves to ensure that I do not take myself too seriously; muddy paws on my skirt matter little (unless I'm on my way to work!) compared to the utter devotion expressed by this bundle of energy. His antics could hardly be called utilitarian by our pragmatic American standards; Luther does not really perform any useful service, or does he?

We seldom think sufficiently about the interrelationship of all of creation in which each expression of life has its own function. By attending to the wonder of creation, perhaps we can learn that God's grace is always greater than that which merely meets the need; God is extravagantly generous in providing what brings us joy, as well.[8]

Guarding our delicate environment is also the responsibility of humans.[9] Daily articles in magazines and newspapers paint a dire situation for our earth, the home God prepared for us. Too often we have taken the mandate to have dominion to mean that we could do whatever we wanted with our environment.[10] Only in recent years have we begun to learn how interconnected and fragile the web of life really is. When we attempt to protect our natural resources and endangered species, we are expressing our love both for creation and those of the human family who will follow us.

School children are some of the most enthusiastic "re-cyclers" these days. Have you ever made the mistake of tossing a used soda can in the trash in the presence of a well-informed and militantly ecological fifth-grader? She will tell you in no uncertain terms what you, personally, are doing to harm Mother Earth. I genuinely hope that these children will teach all of us some new habits as well as carry this commitment into their own adulthood.

Our role as caretakers for the world involves other human beings. Many persons are not capable of caring for themselves. The stronger ones are responsible for caring for the weaker ones: the children, the elderly, the diseased, the forgotten. While the evolution of other species may depend upon instinctual "survival of the fittest," humans are called to preserve and enhance the lives of all, giving special attention to those "least fit" to care for themselves.[11]

Walker Percy's novel, *The Thanatos Syndrome*,[12] is a satire of the "expendable" mindset of much of contemporary society. In one section of the book, Percy talks about society's need for the elderly, the disabled, and those afflicted with Down's syndrome or schizophrenia to be "compassionately eliminated." While each of us would resist such a cheapening of human life, often we unconsciously contribute to such a procedure by the way we allow state or federal governments or charitable organizations to determine how money will be spent. We must not add our complicity to such an expendable approach to human beings.

Another aspect of bearing the image of God is the creativity humans possess. We are like God in this characteristic. Whenever we plant a garden, redecorate a room, compose a sonata, quilt a warm covering for a bed, or make a piece of furniture, the gift of creativity expresses itself. Of course, only God can call creation out of nothing, but humans are gifted with the ability to make something of beauty out of what might appear to many to be useless materials. Through imaginative ideas we can rearrange the raw materials that God provides us. Indeed, what we produce bears the stamp of our own unique identity, just as the world and especially its people reflect God's glory and character. Becoming human involves learning to "read the language of beauty."[13]

God also shares God's own creative capacity with us that "we might be fruitful and multiply," another assignment given to our ancestors. Our presence today shows how seriously they took this responsibility! To plan to conceive a child, a luxury in this world given the inequity of awareness and cultural acceptability concerning contraception, can only be done with belief in the promise of the future. While many couples dread the idea of bringing a child into a world such as ours, those who decide to be parents are obligated to do so as an act of sacred trust and hopeful imagination.

Christ as the Image of God

In the New Testament, the apostle Paul adds a further dimension to our understanding of what it means for humans to be in the "image of God." Here the title refers almost exclusively to Jesus Christ (I Cor 11:7; 2 Cor 4:4; Col 1:15).

Paul used an analogy to describe the significance of Christ's redemptive work by calling Christ "the second Adam." Adam, a generic word for humanity, did not actualize the identity that God intended, but sought rather to allow pride and temporal gratification to distract and, ultimately, distort. Only Christ has lived fully the human life desired by God. One of my teachers, John A. T. Robinson, liked to describe Jesus as the only "normal person who ever lived." By that he meant that everyone else had failed to live up to the dignity and responsibility for which they were created.

Without a great deal of explanation, Paul simply insisted that Jesus alone is the image of God.[14] Jesus fulfills the role God intended for the human being; and the abiding presence of his spirit makes possible that others might follow his example. He serves as God's representative, exercising the proper dominion and leadership meant for human beings. He restores persons whose sin kept them from being free to become fully human.

With Paul's teaching on the image of God, we can conclude that the image of God is not so much something that is given as it is something to be realized.[15] It is a development of character that we can realize through attentive listening to the call of God through the teaching of Christ and compassionate service in his name. In Christ we have received a pattern for our own identities; we must walk in obedience to God as he did in order to reflect the image of God.

One of my favorite short stories is Nathaniel Hawthorne's, *The Great Stone Face*.[16] It tells about a young boy, Ernest, who grew up in the shadow of a remarkable face, composed of a formation of rocks on a mountain overlooking the valley where he lived. Since his childhood, the face had fascinated Ernest, and daily he spent time beholding its benevolent character. A long-standing prophecy among the people said that someday one would come whose face resembled the giant visage. Ernest yearned for that person more than the other inhabitants of his village, for he had grown to love and unconsciously emulate the face from his long practice of studying it with care.

Several renowned men returned to the valley of their birth, and each time the villagers expected that this one would surely fulfill the prophecy. But each time, the people, and Ernest in particular, were disappointed. At long last, a famous poet came to the village, having written about the face and the human who most nearly might correspond to it. In Ernest, he recognized the one who bore the likeness of the Great Stone Face. By his attentive contemplation of the face for all of his life, he had come to reflect its own distinctive character and likeness.

The New Testament invites us to regard Christ "with unveiled faces" that we might be transformed "into his likeness" (2 Cor 3:18). Like Ernest, we will become like that upon which we set our heart. The goal of our lives as human beings is to bear the image of God in Christ. Though all persons share in this potentiality because they are created in the image of God, not all will give themselves to listening intently to the call of God through Christ.

Paul described the true destiny of the human family. It is a pathway that has been marked by Jesus Christ. When we receive him into our lives through faith, a gradual recasting of our personalities occurs that molds us into loving, other-oriented persons. No longer do we merely look to our own interests, but we are concerned for the well-being of those around us (Phil 2:4). Our lives are inclined toward service and stewardship, our original job description. Becoming human, then, is not restoration to the state prior to the Edenic fall. It is participation in the new creation.

Revelation of God through the Image

Earlier I noted that God's creation tells us something about the creator. As we know, any work of art unmistakably points to dimensions in the identity of the artist. We can trace recurring patterns in the compositions of Ludwig Beethoven or the paintings of Marc Chagall that illumine the context in which the artists worked or the personal triumph or travail they had experienced. Especially in their later works, Beethoven's deafness and Chagall's preoccupation with human suffering provide the subtexts of their contributions.

We humans, who uniquely image God in creation, also tell something about the One who formed us. Thus, the image of God borne by humans can be a window through which to glimpse contours of the character of God. Of course, the grace and grandeur of God can never be fully expressed by a human, even though the Bible speaks of Jesus as the one in whom "the fullness of deity dwells bodily" (Col 2:9). Yet, for the "Word to be made flesh" implies a necessary self-limitation for, though God can be present, God cannot be contained in any finite structure.

Even so, we can learn about God through those who have cultivated their likeness to God. But how can we recognize such? A person cultivates his or her "likeness to God" not only through the contemplation of God, but also through expressing concern for those for whom God is most concerned. The prophets of the Old Testament ringingly declared that God is on the side of the poor, the widow, and the orphan.[17] Further, they stated that God is concerned about those whom Israel might regard as "foreign." God's grace is much wider than the arbitrary boundaries set up by persons claiming the "preferential option."

Bearing the image of God, then, must mean that one is committed to ethical activity on behalf of the oppressed.[18] As one's life gives evidence of genuine concern for just relations with others, she or he is reflecting the justice of God. Those committed to the care of others "in Jesus' name" are indeed reminders of the love God feels toward all persons.

Mother Theresa wrote of encountering Jesus in the poor persons with whom she ministered. Caring for them was an expression of her love for her savior. We can also say that those persons who received her generous care learned of the compassion of God for them through her. She communicated to them through her presence that God has not forgotten them and does not will to abandon them. Indeed, perhaps the chief distinctive of the image of God is that we are allowed to be the expression of God's compassion and care in the world. Persons are better able to believe our words about faith in God when we live as if our belief really does make a difference. The image of God is restored in us as we live in the imitation of Christ.

As God's representatives in the world, equipped with much freedom (and curiosity!) to explore the wonder of this universe, our discoveries point to a creator of infinite wisdom and creativity. Those persons who presently display the most profound sense of wonder about our world (and perhaps about the one who brought it forth) are not the theologians, apparently, but the scientists.[19] Their sophisticated attempts to understand the structure and origins of the space we inhabit reveal an even greater order and purpose than previously imagined. As their discoveries further illumine the vastness of their inquiry, they are driven to ask questions about God. Many scientists realize that their own competence for such an immense undertaking is determined by the creator who welcomes this extension of human "dominion."

As God's handiwork, the human reveals much of God's intent for this world, which has the promise of interdependent harmony, with care being the primary sustaining impulse. The human has the responsibility of managing this delicate balance as God's own representative.

Community Necessary to the Image of God

The Bible carefully states that the human was not created in the image of God as an isolated individual. No one can be a human alone. We do not give birth to ourselves, nor can we mature as persons without interaction with others and our creator. The Genesis passage notes that humans bear the image of God in community; the primal form of this community is as male and female,[20] but is not limited to that.

In earlier years, biblical interpreters saw in the plural "let us make" a suggestion of God as trinity. While this interpretation is probably reading too much into the text, we are not wrong to think that persons are like God in that they are fully personal by existing in relationship. The Christian faith confesses that God is eternally trinitarian, living in the richness of mutuality and relationship within the being of God.[21]

Bearing the image of God requires that we live in self-giving interdependent relationships as does our God. Just as God was willing to draw humanity into the very being of God through the sending and raising of Jesus Christ, so must we create space in our lives for those without community.

One of Rudyard Kipling's *Just So Stories* is entitled "The Cat Who Walked by Himself." It is a humorous account of feline obstinacy and the pretension of human self-sufficiency. Of course, some persons may need to live a more solitary existence than others, but most persons do not thrive in such a situation. Our true identities are formed as we offer ourselves in commitment to others for the common good.

Two of my friends, both in their sixties, are now the legal guardians of an African adolescent. The girl was in their city for burn therapy and could not return home without threatening the progress of her treatment. She needed someone with whom she could stay, persons who would assist her family in providing the necessary care. My friends learned of her plight and decided to offer their aid. They invited her to live with them for as long as she needed. By drawing the girl into their family, they are revealers of the love of God and are making possible a relationship in which she can cultivate the image of God herself.

The Image of God as a Future Possession

I have spoken of the image of God being formed, cultivated, and pursued. Obviously, we must experience a process to become fully what we are created to be. We are also reminded that only Christ was fully the image of God during his human life. The image of God is a potentiality that is given to each of us as God's creation, but it is only realized as we learn of our kinship to Christ and our need of his salvation.

Thus, we need to remember that the image of God is a call to each human being. The call comes to us in a variety of ways: through our perception that we were created to live in caring relations to others, through the words of scripture, and through our contemplation of the wonder of this world. It comes to us in ways tailored to our unique individual experience.

James Fowler, a professor at Emory University, has written about "stages of faith."[22] He argues, quite effectively, that persons grow in their faith along some fairly predictable pathways. One's psychological and emotional maturity determines, in large measure, how one develops in her or his spiritual understanding and actions. Fowler demonstrates the process by which humans become self-transcending in their concern for God and others. He notes, also, how few persons pursue their full calling as persons through whom God desires to embrace the world. Their humanity remains impoverished because of this neglect.

In conclusion, the image of God has both physical and spiritual dimensions. Humans have the capacity to reason and lead the rest of creation. They also are created to respond to God with openness and obedience. Bearing the image of God can be likened to a journey. One may have a vague idea of the ultimate destiny at the beginning, but only the intermediate stops along the way clarify where the travel will really end. Humans must be resigned to the reality that we are limited to only a partial reflection of the image of God in this life. Our true selves are bound up with the Christ, however, and we walk in hope.

I believe that if we consciously regard ourselves as persons created to bear the image of God, our sense of what it means to be human will be transformed. Bearing the image of God is a far loftier calling than most of us realize. It is never fitting to say that we are only human. To become human is a wonderful opportunity that will take our best efforts throughout our lives.

Endnotes

[1]David Cairns, *The Image of God in Man* (London: SCM Press, 1953) gives a comprehensive survey of biblical and theological understandings of *imago dei*. Though somewhat dated, its historical overview remains helpful. More timely is the work (cited previously) by Douglas John Hall, *Imaging God*.

[2]Edmund Hill, *Being Human: A Biblical Perspective* (London: Geoffrey Chapman, 1984) 197, suggests that the idea of humans as the image of God is not simply concerned to tell us something about ourselves, but also something about God.

[3]Jürgen Moltmann, *God in Creation* (San Francisco: Harper & Row, 1985) 219, describes this responsibility as representing God on earth. "The human being is God's indirect manifestation on earth."

[4]Hendrikus Berkhof, *Christian Faith*, rev. ed. (Grand Rapids MI: Eerdmans, 1986) 186-87, speaks of the "answering character" of the human as "respondable." Barth stresses a similar theme.

[5]This does not mean a privatized encounter of the individual with God. Rather, in the piercing words of Margaret Miles, "A life before God in our time requires a degree

of social responsibility far greater than that recognized by most historical Christian writers." See her *Practicing Christianity: Critical Perspectives for an Embodied Spirituality* (New York: Crossroad, 1990) 2.

[6]"Man," counsels Dostoevski's Father Zosima, "love the animals.... Do not pride yourself on your superiority to the animals, they are without sin." *The Brothers Karamazov,* trans. Constance Garnett (London: Wm. Heinemann Ltd., 1912) 332. See also James Sarpell, *In the Company of Animals: A Study of Human-Animal Relationships* (London: Basil Blackwell, 1986).

[7]Moltmann, 188, observes that this act of naming is not simply an act of rule; rather "it brings animals into a community of language with human beings."

[8]In *To Work and To Love* (Fortress Press: Philadelphia, 1984) 49, Dorothee Sölle writes, "A spirituality of creation reminds us that we were born for joy."

[9]See the essay by Conrad Bonifazi, "Biblical Roots of an Ecologic Conscience," in *This Little Planet,* ed. Michael Hamilton (New York: Charles Scribner's Sons, 1970) especially 226-27.

[10]Rosemary Radford Ruether underscores the anthropocentric view of nature that has been commonplace until the 1970s. *See Gaia and God* (New York: Harper Collins, 1992) 218ff.

[11]Douglas John Hall, *Imaging God: Dominion as Stewardship* (Grand Rapids Ml: Eerdmans, 1986) 151, writes: "The imaging of God in our relations with one another must mean that every human being is called to take upon himself/herself the service of the other."

[12]Walker Percy, *The Thanatos Syndrome* (New York: Farrar, Straus, & Giroux, 1987).

[13]Hans Urs Von Balthasar, *The Glory of the Lord: A Theological Aesthetics,* trans. E. Leiva-Merikakis (New York: Crossroad, 1982) 19.

[14]A. T. Hanson, *The Image of the Invisible God* (London: SCM Press, 1982) 104, shares Robinson's perspective in the statement: "We can say that in Jesus Christ we have the God-given model for the new humanity."

[15]In the revised edition of Frank Stagg's *Polarities of Human Existence* (Macon GA: Smyth & Helwys Publishing, Inc., 1994) 84, Stagg writes: "We are made to become but we cannot become through ourselves alone."

[16]In *The Complete Novels and Selected Tales,* ed. Norman Holmes Pearson (New York: The Modern Library, 1937).

[17]E.g., Isa 58:6-8; Amos 5:12-15; Micah 2:1-11.

[18]Working for justice is the sign of Christ's presence in the church, according to Letty M. Russell in *Church in the Round* (Louisville: Westminster/John Knox, 1993) 127ff.

[19]E.g., James Trefil, *The Moment of Creation* (New York: Scribners, 1983) and Stephen Hawking, *A Brief History of Time* (New York: Bantam Books, 1988).

[20]As you may recall, Karl Barth grounded human sexuality in the *imago dei*, but renders it as an "unequal duality." His treatment is found in *Church Dogmatics*, III/I, 41, pts. 2, 3, trans. J.W. Edwards, D. Bussey, and H. Knight (Edinburgh: T & T Clark, 1958).

[21]Catherine M. LaCugna, *God for Us* (New York: Harper Collins, 1991) 246, writes: the "mysteries of human personhood and communion have their origin and destiny in God's personal [trinitarian] existence."

[22]A ground-breaking study, James Fowler employs extensive empirical research in constructing a theory of growth in faith. See his *Stages of Faith* (San Francisco: Harper & Row, 1981).

The Redemption of Humanity

So far we have talked about what it means to be human in terms of our distinctive origin with God as our creator and what it means to be created in the "image of God." Now we need to examine our common human experience as sinful creatures, as people who fail to live up to the marvelous potentiality given us in creation. Questions such as "What is sin?" "What are the consequences of sin?" "Does sin ruin a person forever?" "How can sinful human beings reach their true identity?" will guide our reflection in this chapter.

All human beings know that something has gone wrong in our world. Surely God did not mean for people to live as age-old enemies, armed to the teeth, with military forces just daring a rival to pick a fight. We claim to love peace, but as we review our own government's budget, we realize our real priorities. Our eyes widen when we compare what we spend on bombs and what we spend on bread for the hungry. We have strayed from the pathway God purposed for us, and we need to be brought back. I do not believe it is possible for anyone to save himself or herself; God alone can do that. We are "broke, too broke to mend," in the words of the poet John Masefield. Only the one who made us can make possible our re-creation.

What is Sin?

"Sin" is a rather old-fashioned word, belonging more to the world of religious belief than to the world of psychology or politics. The powerful preaching of our American Puritan forebear Jonathan Edwards, who prompted sweeping conversions through his terrifying image of "sinners in the hands of an angry God," can no longer command the attention of contemporary people. For that reason, many persons would rather describe the human condition in less condemning language.

Sensing this modern reframing, the famed psychiatrist Karl Menninger wrote a provocative book entitled *Whatever Became of Sin?* He noted that by abandoning the category of "sin," Americans have not really been able to relieve themselves of guilt. Rather, their feelings of contradiction and insecurity are now simply interpreted in different terms, usually psychological or sociological. Menninger stressed that this was no solution because some actions can only be correctly described when we call them sin.[1]

Sin has a distinctively theological meaning.[2] In biblical terms, it is the deliberate violation of the known will of God. The specific sin might be refusing to honor God, a betrayal of another person, or a distortion of our true identity. The Bible offers many examples of human sinfulness and its consequences. The story of Adam and Eve in the garden is the most familiar of these, but it is not the only biblical example of human sinfulness, as we shall see as we examine several different texts. But we should begin with the story of the "forbidden fruit."

Most of us are so well acquainted with the major points of this story that we assume there is nothing left to learn. We already have our minds made up about culprits and the serpentine villain. Try to listen one more time to this foundational understanding of "what went wrong," remembering that this story is one among others.

What did Adam and Eve actually do that forced them to start looking for a new place to live, driven out of Eden? After arriving on the scene, our ancestors were given a job description that included taking care of one another and the garden. Only one thing did God specifically forbid: they were not to eat from "the tree of the knowledge of good and evil" (Gen 2:17). There is perhaps no more enigmatic a phrase in scripture than this. God had told Adam and Eve that they could eat from all of the other trees in the garden, but this one was strictly off-limits. I think it is helpful to think of the sin described in this story as the root sin of all.[3] "Taking something that didn't belong to them," as some interpreters have described their action, hardly gives the full picture. Nor does the idea that the essence of sin is disobedience to a commandment from God tell the whole story. Simply eating the apple —in South Africa they call it a peach—was not the cause of what later theologians describe as "the fall." The action was much more serious than that.

The temptation scene in Genesis 3 offers an interpretation of the true nature of sin. Sin is refusing to live within the limitations set by God. Neither the woman nor the serpent accurately recalled the commandment of God, and they surely misunderstood its motive.[4] When questioned by the crafty serpent about God's command, Eve spoke more about the unpleasant consequence of disobeying God than the breaking of relationship through willful disobedience. Many of us are like Eve; we worry more about "getting caught" than whether or not an action is right or wrong in God's sight.

The serpent further compounded the inattentiveness to God's instruction by suggesting that it was not really dangerous to eat of the tree, after all. The tempter suggested that God was actually deceiving the human beings by forbidding them to eat from the tree because God was secretly worried that they might become as wise as God. The serpent subtly hinted that God could not be trusted and was selfish. The woman believed the twisted half-truth of the tempter and decided that the fruit of the tree actually did belong to them. She ate of it and offered it to her husband, who unquestioningly joined her in defying God. By their willingness to believe the tempter and to distrust God, our human parents showed us the essence of sin: a turning away from God to some supposed greater good. Thus, the source and root of all sin is the self-deluding idea that we know better than God, and that we are really answerable to no one.[5]

I do not think that we should make too much of the story's attribution of the first sin to Eve. Christian tradition has used this aspect of the narrative to condemn women as the source of sin and, therefore, to preclude them from equal dignity with men, especially as it relates to vocation in ministry. Actually, the command against eating of the tree was given to the man before the creation of woman, as the writer of Genesis 2 sketches the story. The woman's prominent role in the conversation with the serpent and the man's complicity with her is the author's way of making sure we know that both of them were involved.[6] This, then, is the story of all human sin with neither gender to be blamed as more at fault than the other.

What was the motive for the first act of rebellion? Dietrich Bonhoeffer, a German martyr for opposing the ruthless action of Hitler in the second world war, described the sin of Adam and Eve as refusing to live within the limits or the boundary set by God.[7] They wanted to be God, not creatures dependent upon and responsible to their creator. The motivation for their action was pride. They wanted to know everything and "be as God." "Knowledge of good and of evil" is a Hebrew phrase that means unlimited knowledge. Thus, the tree in the center of the garden stood for the kind of knowledge only God can possess.

Scripture speaks frequently about the wisdom "from above" granted by God (James 1:5; 3:15). Such wisdom cannot be snatched away from God, but received as a gracious gift. God desires that we ask for wisdom and is pleased to grant it, just as the young king Solomon's request was honored.[8]

Human beings find great difficulty in asking for what we need. As infants, we scream unintelligibly our requests; as grown-ups, we either pretend that we are capable of meeting all of our needs or simply do not know what they are or how to ask for them.

I have always wondered why Adam and Eve did not ask God more about the tree.[9] Surely they had to be puzzled about the significance of the one tree that was forbidden to them. Why was it singled out as hazardous to their health? As we recall, the warning was that they "would surely die" on that day when they might eat from it. Were they afraid to ask, fearing that their creator would be upset with them for questioning the divine command? Or were they overly confident of their ability to obey perfectly? "Sure, God, no problem, anything you say."

Have you ever thought that God might have wanted them to question the command? That would have provided a "teachable moment" for God to share with them further about their identity and their destiny. They might have learned that, rather than being selfish with knowledge about the world and the divine purpose in it, God desired to share with them how they could grow in wisdom as God's responsible partners.

Some things are pointless to tell others, however, until they demonstrate a willingness to hear. Evidently Adam and Eve had no interest in the "why" of the command. Not until I was stranded on the side of the road with a flat tire as a teenage girl did I really know I needed my daddy's "Simple Mechanics for the Uninformed Daughter" course that he had been insisting I needed to take. After my calamity, I was patient enough to listen to his instruction.

Sin, then, is not only pride, pretending to be utterly self-sufficient and thus trying to replace God in our lives. It might also be underestimating our dignity and responsibility as God's special creatures. Rather than thinking too much of myself as a human being, this expression of sin would be to think too little.[10] Many of us suffer from this unwillingness to take ourselves seriously enough. Sin can only be understood when we remember the meaning of being created in the image of God.

Other texts in scripture describe the character of sin. Because it stands at the beginning of the biblical canon, Genesis offers several instances of sin as a way of introducing us to the idea that this entire collection of books is about the redemption of wayward human beings. Two other passages in Genesis outline the contours of our sinfulness.

The story of the Flood tells the result of when human wickedness becomes unrestrainable (Gen 6-9). As we teach children of God's rescue of Noah, his family, and the animals, our focus is usually more on God's preservation of the human race and the other creatures than on the judgment of the devastating flood. Indeed, that is reason for its inclusion in the Bible, but it is a story of both grace and judgment.

We must not overlook the tragic dimension of the strained relationship with God caused by the rampant sinning of human beings. Further, our sinful actions do not harm us alone; they contribute to the sinning of other human beings, all of which bring cataclysmic results for the rest of God's creatures. When we refuse to live as God's responsible stewards, all of creation suffers.[11] Genesis 9:2 reminds us of the disruption sin brings: "The fear and dread of you shall rest on every animal of the earth."

The tale of the tower of Babel is like the story of Adam and Eve in that it portrays our unwillingness to live with limits as human beings. Again, pride propelled the activity of ambitious people. In building the tower, reaching toward the heavens, they were concerned about making "a name for themselves" (Gen 11:4). Again, God frustrated the plans of people who insisted upon defining their own identity through turning away from their creator.

During a visit to New York City, I was struck with the desire for predominance and acclaim evident in the design and structure of the larger buildings. We have our own versions of the tower of Babel in striving to outdo all the competitors by having the tallest, most opulently decorated, unparalleled architectural lines. People still try to make a name for themselves in this manner.

The New Testament takes a somewhat different approach in describing our human sinfulness. It vividly points out how we miss the mark by contrasting our lives with the life of Jesus Christ, who was "tested as we are, yet without sin" (Heb 4:15). Indeed, only in the light of the full faithfulness of Jesus can we understand our distance from God's intent.

Through the proclamation and example of Jesus, we learn that it is not good enough to be "religious" if our hearts are cold toward those in need (Matt 12:9-14). Sounding the themes of the great prophets of Israel (Isa 58), Jesus warned that acts of piety count for little if we have no compassion or mercy. Those who despise the "little ones" show themselves to be no friend of God (Luke 18:15-17). Likewise, Jesus punctured the pomposity of those of us who pride ourselves on our generosity—he pointed out that we only care for those who are of our race and economic level (Matt 5:46-48). Our sin consists not only in what we do against God and others, but what we fail to do in their behalf.

The stories of courageous persons who rescued Jews from the Holocaust show us the cost of acting in behalf of others. Persons facing persecution were aided not by the refusal of Christians to participate in their incarceration, but by those who actively resisted the actions of the Nazis through hiding and transporting Jews in their hour of need.[12]

Jesus reserved a special condemnation for those who presumed they were God's favorites. None of us should call "unclean" what God has called "clean," which means acceptable and welcome as a part of God's family.[13] The apostle Peter struggled, like many of us, to learn this truth about God and all of God's people (Acts 10:9-29).

The apostle Paul gave us further insight about the nature of sin by accenting the role that the law of God plays (Rom 7:9-11). By his own testimony, he reminded us that something within us longs for what is forbidden. It is not a pretty truth about us—what lies just outside our reach seems more attractive to us than what is properly ours. We covet what belongs to God and to other persons. Paul described human sinfulness in its tendency to want to transgress the law; that is why the law is so powerful . . . and also why no one can be justified through trying to keep the law. The law incites our rebellion and condemns our disobedience.[14]

Three terms summarize the biblical view of sin, ungodliness (Ps 119:163; Rom 1:18), idolatry (Exod 20:3-4), and estrangement from God and others (Eph 4:18). These terms describe a comprehensive and personal disorder. It is a larger problem than the wrong things that we do; rather it has to do with being inclined in a direction other than what God intended. Actions displeasing to God and harmful to others and ourselves flow out of being turned away from God.

Are All People Sinful?

It has been said that more evidence is given in the Bible for the doctrine of sin than any other doctrine of the church. I agree. The Bible tells us not only that all of us are sinful (I John 1:8), but that we are each somehow aware that we have failed to live as we ought and that we need forgiveness. This knowledge of our sinfulness is not confined to those of us who consider ourselves Christians, but is shared by all human beings. Whether we describe this awareness as "feeling guilty" or a lack of satisfaction with our lives, we are so constructed that we cannot live at cross-purposes with our potentiality as the image of God without suffering discomfort.

Why are all people sinful? Are we simply born that way, or is it purely voluntary? We could spend the rest of our lives reading the multitude of books that have been written on this topic, for the universal expression of sin among people has troubled many.

Two early Christian thinkers, Pelagius and Augustine, debated this very question, and we usually look to them for a clear statement of the problem. Pelagius, a British monk who taught in Rome during the late fourth and early fifth centuries, argued that sin is purely voluntary and that every person begins with the same degree of innocence and freedom as Adam and Eve.[15] According to Pelagius, if we sin, we only have ourselves to blame. While our human ancestors may have set a bad example, they are not responsible for our wrong choices.

Augustine, Bishop of Hippo in North Africa and the leading Christian thinker of his day, strongly argued just the opposite. "If we believe that sin is purely voluntary," he reasoned, "then why is everyone a sinner?" We must inherit an evil nature that determines that we will all sin, he concluded.[16]

Augustine painted a glorious picture of Adam in the garden prior to his "fall." God intended him to be eternally young, immune from physical injury, and full of spiritual goodness. He had the capacity not to die, if he had just continued in the direction he was created to go. But along with Eve, Adam gave in to the temptation of the serpent and thereby plunged the whole human race into sin. All people are automatically included in Adam's sin because as the father of the human race, we were "in his loins." Thus, when we are born, we are tainted with original sin transmitted through our parents, which is both an inherited guilt and an irrevocable inclination to do evil. This is the background to the phrase children learned in the early American primers: "In Adam's fall, we sinned all."

Obviously, each of these versions concerning human sinfulness contains some truth, but neither Pelagius nor Augustine offered a sufficiently balanced view. We do not start at the same place as Adam and Eve, contrary to Pelagius' position. There is a whole history of sinning prior to our personal contribution of our own not very "original" sin. We are born into a world that has been distorted through generations of persons unwilling to live within the limits set by God.[17] It is a world capable of rejecting and killing the Son of God, the one sent to redeem us.

On the other hand, we are not guilty for what our human ancestors did, as Augustine argued. We cannot blame them for our misdeeds. The story of Adam and Eve is the story of every human being; it is your story and my story. The apostle Paul gave a more comprehensive picture than either Pelagius or Augustine. He asserted the unity and solidarity of human beings in sin—we are all "Adam"—and yet maintained that we each remain directly responsible (Rom 5:12-21; 1 Cor 15:21-22).

What are the Consequences of Sin?

As we have noted, being a sinful person is more a state of rebellion against God than any specific act. Resistance to God's purpose for us, which is the "Sin," results in "sins." Not only is our relationship to God disrupted through our pride and unbelief, but we no longer live with others or nature in the harmony of the "garden." We exploit others, trying to dominate them and bring them under our control.

The sensual aspects of our bodies such as our desires for food, sexual expression, and nice clothing—good gifts from God that make us fully human—grow wildly out of control as our appetites become insatiable. We want it all, now. Lust, greed, gluttony, and workaholism pull us along like some marionette controlled by strings in the hands of another. One early Christian writer warned his flock against "forging a chain of habit." Incidental acts that really do not seem too bad by themselves can become habitual expressions of self-destruction from which escape is most difficult.

I saw a full-page advertisement for "Cocaine Anonymous" in the *New York Times*. It was a first-person account of a prominent attorney who became hooked on cocaine and consequently lost his practice, family, and community standing. The addiction to drugs began almost casually as he asked his pharmacist for something to "pick him up" so that he could continue his excessive work habits. Soon he needed something to calm him down from the effects of the amphetamines, and then he discovered that most seductive drug, cocaine, which began to control his life.

Debts mounted, the family disintegrated, and he was charged with supplying drugs to minors in his neighborhood. His misery and desperation finally drove him to ask God to help him seek treatment for his addiction, from which he is slowly recovering. He is telling his story to warn all of us of the dangers of experimenting with drugs, hoping that others might avoid his destructive path.

Paul maintained that "the wages of sin is death," which he interpreted primarily in a spiritual sense as being separated from God. We can either be living in the direction of death or in the direction of eternal life. Thus, the time of biological death ratifies the direction we have been heading.[18] Many persons are already living in a kind of hell of their own making, as this man's story reveals.

My grandmother had a saying: "Virtue is its own reward." I suppose all grandmothers claim that adage. She meant for us to learn that doing the right thing has a built-in satisfaction. In the same way, wrong-doing has some inescapable misery in it. We worry about being "found out," we live with a vague uneasiness that we try to push to the back of our minds, and we keep trying to rationalize our behavior. I believe that reaping these internal consequences from our sins is the main way we experience God's judgment. Of course, when we break the law, the civil government becomes the means God uses to punish us.

We do not cease to be human when we sin, even though our true identity becomes distorted.[19] Some of the great debates in the history of the church have to do with the extent of our depravity, a favorite word in many Protestant confessions. I have found it helpful to think of our sinfulness in an extensive rather than an intensive way, which simply means that while we are not as "bad" as we can be, no part of us is untouched by our rebellion against God.[20] We increasingly become aware that we are never free from mixed motives; even our acts of charity are colored by self-serving concerns. The freedom to obey God without struggle is not our experience.

How does God respond to our sin? We often do not think that our actions are capable of affecting God, but the Bible speaks of

God's sorrow, anger, and mercy as divine responses to our neglect of God's will. Our actions matter greatly to God. Many of us focus only on the emotion of anger, believing that no matter how hard we try, we can never please our demanding, perfectionist Creator. Although the Bible does speak of God's wrath, which refers to God's displeasure and the punishment our actions draw forth, the primary accent of scripture is upon the mercy of our God. We need to recover this truth that is at the heart of learning to believe that God is for us.

How Can We Reach Our True Identity?

All of us are sinful people with broken promises, broken dreams, and a broken spirit. Our efforts to "do better" ebb into discouragement as we realize how little power we have to change our lives in our own strength. We understand why some interpreters of the human situation have little hope that we can ever fulfill our true destiny.[21]

The Bible does not only tell of human failure, but speaks of God's unwillingness to let us go our own way indefinitely. The most moving part of the Adam and Eve saga is the action of God after they transgressed the divine command.[22] God was looking for them, giving them an opportunity to confess their wrong. As we recall, neither wanted to take his or her full responsibility, preferring to pass the blame. Even so, God provided for them the clothing they would need for their harsher form of living "east of Eden."

In many ways, this picture of God providing a "covering" for those sinful humans is a summary of all the divine action for our redemption. God provides a way for us to learn that God's final word to us is not of judgment, but of mercy. God does not abandon us, but creatively finds ways to bridge the separation caused by our sin. The gracious attitude of God toward the sinner is clearly presented in Jesus' parable of the prodigal son (Luke 15). We love this story so much because it shows God's patience with our errant ways and the glad welcome waiting for us if we will return from our "far countries." It also shows the great joy God has when we believe our true home is found in the security of this relationship.[23]

It is harder in our day to make assumptions about how people feel about the distinctly religious theme of redemption. Gone are the days when we could assume that everybody "believes in God" and somehow feels accountable to our divine maker. Many people express, however, a deep threat and fear in their lives that nothing seems to take away. No wonder we can observe the rampant growth in self-help remedies and therapeutic approaches—which indicates that many of us are searching for something! I would call that "something" redemption.

Perhaps the best way I can describe the experience of redemption is when a human being can really believe in a new beginning. The New Testament uses the term "born again" to describe the new life that God will grant to those who ask. Different circumstances can bring us to the point of asking for God's forgiveness and direction, but few of us will ask before we sense our need of what God offers or before we are convinced that we cannot live this life without divine help.

God offers to us a savior and a friend. Jesus Christ spent his whole life showing and telling people who felt far away from God that they had a special invitation to enter the new order being established by God. He told them how simple it was to enter this new realm: to believe in God and the One sent by God (John 17:3). Believing in Jesus meant for them and for us a new life of discipleship characterized by generosity, kindness, and unflinching trust in the care of God. This new life would be evident in a new willingness to lay down their lives for others, just as Jesus offered his life for the redemption of all the world. We cannot follow Jesus without learning to love all that he desires to embrace.[24]

When we receive Christ, we also receive a new family of brothers and sisters whose destiny is bound with ours. Redemption is never a private act. We are not just changed on the inside, but are given a new way of relating to others. Jesus' life is our model for establishing accepting, merciful, intimate human relationships.[25]

A few years ago our church welcomed into its membership a middle-aged man who had long considered the questions of faith. Making a commitment to God was not an easy matter for Howard, and he had said if he ever took that step, he wanted it to be life-changing. Finally our friend was able to confess his faith in Christ and receive Christian baptism. The transformation in this man has been remarkable as he tries to let his actions reflect his new life of faith. Always a shy, rather non-communicative individual, he has begun to greet people with warmth and genuine affection. He talks about how he approaches his profession with new enthusiasm and a deep concern for those with whom he works. His expressions of faith are reminding all of us of the concrete changes Christ can bring about in our lives. Redemption is not just about the future; rather it enables us to live in new dimensions in the present.

Only by receiving this savior can we become who God intended for us to be. Thus, redemption is more than retreading a former identity. Paul described the life in Christ as a "new creation" (2 Cor 5:17), which means we have been granted a new life with eternal possibilities.[26] No longer striving to gain God's approval or fearful of death, we are liberated to live in fully human ways on this earth with the assured hope that our lives have enduring significance.

Liberation from Sinfulness

The transformation of our identity, so that our lives become more and more like Jesus, is a gradual process. Of course, some Christians will make more steady progress in this endeavor than others. We must remember, however, that the Christian life does not depend upon what we achieve, but upon what we are willing to receive, as one contemporary spiritual director has written.

Therefore, we are to cultivate a willingness to listen for all of the ways in which God will speak to us.

Just as we receive our redemption through God's grace, so will our lives come to reflect the life of Jesus through grace. One stanza in Luther's hymn "A Mighty Fortress" states,

> Did we in our own strength confide,
> our striving would be losing;
> Were not the right Man on our side,
> the Man of God's own choosing.

The liberation we experience from our bondage to sinfulness is through the ever-present help of our Savior who is much more patient with us than we are with ourselves. As a monk, Luther learned that one can only be justified by faith; good works are not enough. Trying to live perfectly before God drove him to the edge of his sanity. "Who can please a righteous God?" he muttered. This beloved hymn expresses Luther's gratitude that he had been set free from trying to earn his redemption.

No doubt we will grow impatient when we stumble in the same areas repeatedly, but we must not despair. God promises to be our companion for life, willing to offer guidance and encouragement if we will seek it. Nothing can separate us from God's redeeming love.

Further, we do not have to flee this world to draw near to God. As human beings, we are created for this world and can best learn the ways of God through the ongoing history God has with this world. Redemption is for the whole person in community, and it involves all of creation.

As we become more intently turned toward God, rather than turned away, we will be able to exercise the responsible care for our world and its creatures that God desires. Our liberation from sin will positively affect the rest of creation, for it will no longer be the victim of exploitation because of our selfish interests.

Endnotes

[1]Karl Menninger, *Whatever Became of Sin?* (New York: Hawthorn Books, 1973).

[2]See the fine study by David L. Smith, *With Willful Intent: A Theology of Sin* (Wheaton IL: Bridge Point, 1994).

[3]In the words of Martin Luther, "The root and source of sin is unbelief," *Luther's Works*, 1:162, 34:155.

[4]Interpreters customarily have taken great liberties in their commentary on this passage. See Elaine Pagels, *Adam, Eve, and the Serpent* (New York: Random House, 1988) for a survey of approaches in early Christianity.

[5]Reinhold Niebuhr, *The Nature and Destiny of Man*, 2 vols. (New York: Charles Scribner's Sons, 1941) contends that sin arises because of anxiety experienced by humans. When we attempt to evade this anxiety by denying our finitude and securing our own lives, we sin. Pedro Trigo, *Creation and History*, trans. R. B. Barr (Maryknoll NY: Orbis, 1991) 129, echoes Niebuhr's analysis; Trigo writes: "We find the evil of insecurity bound up with sin."

[6]See the helpful insights of Phyllis Trible, *God and the Rhetoric of Sexuality* (Philadelphia: Fortress Press, 1978) 113ff.

[7]Dietrich Bonhoeffer, *Creation and Fall, Temptation: Two Biblical Studies* (New York: Macmillan, 1958) 52ff.

[8]I Kgs 3:5-12.

[9]As you recall, there were two trees, the "tree of life" and the "tree of knowledge of good and evil"; it is the latter with which the narrative is concerned. Claus Westermann, *Genesis 1-11*, Trans. John J. Scullion, S.J. (Minneapolis: Augsburg, 1984) 211-25, after offering an extended commentary on the significance of the trees, concludes that God's prohibition is the ground of freedom to choose.

[10]See Judith Plaskow, *Sex, Sin and Grace: Women's Experience and the Theologies of Reinhold Niebuhr and Paul Tillich* (Lanham MD: University Press of America, 1980).

[11]The rescue from the flood is the occasion of the "noachic covenant," a covenant with God in which all humanity shares. See John Baillie, *The Idea of Revelation in Recent Thought* (New York: Columbia University Press, 1956) 125f.

[12]The fine new study by my colleague David P. Gushee, *The Righteous Gentiles of the Holocaust: A Christian Interpretation* (Minneapolis: Augsburg Fortress, 1994) examines the activity of "Christian rescuers" on behalf of Jewish victims during the Holocaust.

[13]Paul R. Sponheim, *Faith and the Other: A Relational Theology* (Minneapolis: Fortress Press, 1993) maintains that our lives as humans are constituted by our relationships with that which is other, both God and other humans.

[14]I have been helped greatly in my understanding of Paul's interpretation of the Law by the studies of N. T. Wright, *The Climax of the Covenant* (Minneapolis: Fortress Press, 1991).

[15]Pelagius, "Letter to Demetrias," in *Theological Anthropology*, trans./ed. J. Patout Burns, S.J. (Philadelphia: Fortress Press, 1981) 39-55.

[16]Augustine, "On the Grace of Christ," in *Theological Anthropology*, especially 95-96.

[17]Piet Schoonenberg, S.J., *Man and Sin*, trans. Joseph Donceel, S.J. (Notre Dame IN: University of Notre Dame Press, 1965) 181-82, describes this reality as "being situated" in a world that has compromised human freedom to choose the good.

[18]Karl Rahner describes human death as the occasion when a person utters a final "yes" or "no" to God's grace. See *Foundations of Christian Faith* (New York: Crossroad, 1978) 97-104.

[19]Ted Peters, *God—The World's Future* (Minneapolis: Fortress Press, 1992) 155, describes the effects of sin as "unbecoming." Marjorie H. Suchocki, *The Fall to Violence* (New York: Continuum, 1994) suggests that sin violates all relations and leads to violent chaos.

[20]This is the language employed by Thomas Finger, *Christian Theology: An Eschatological Approach*, vol. 2 (Scottdale PA: Herald Press, 1989).

[21]It is important for us to reclaim Irenaeus' insight that our true fulfillment as humans does not lie in the past in some supposed paradisiacal perfection, but in the future identity we will know in Christ. See his foundational work *Against Heresies*, The Ante-Nicene Fathers, 1:543.

[22]As Wendy Farley, *Tragic Vision and Divine Compassion* (Louisville KY Westminster/John Knox, 1990) 99, movingly writes: "Divine love as the source of a tragic world order is also the source or the vision of . . . compassion that transcends tragedy." See her helpful attempt at a contemporary theodicy.

[23]Edmund Hill, *Being Human* (London: Geoffrey Chapman, 1984) 243, believes that this relationship, to be authentic, must be undertaken in freedom which is the result of God's liberating grace.

[24]Marcus Borg, *Jesus: A New Vision* (San Francisco: Harper & Row, 1987) suggests that following Jesus as a disciple will require a "politics of compassion" that draws us toward others rather than a "politics of holiness" by which we distance ourselves from the "impure."

[25]Nouwen, Henri, Donald McNeill, Douglas Morrison, *Compassion: A Reflection on the Christian Life* (New York: An Image Book, 1988).

[26]Boyd Hunt, beloved theology professor at Southwestern Baptist Theological Seminary, stresses that redemption is best viewed from an eschatological perspective. His volume, *Redeemed! Eschatological Redemption and the Kingdom of God* (Nashville: Broadman & Holmann, 1993) provides a systematic theology of redemption.

The Duality of Humanity

Chapter 4

"[And God] created them male and female" (Gen 1:27). As human persons, we are either female or male, as this foundational verse in scripture declares. Even before we were born, our parents were deciding on names and dreaming about how we might look and what we might become. From the moment that we bellow our own birth announcement, our biological sex determines, in many ways, how persons surrounding us will respond. We cannot help but relate as female or male, the biological given of one's personhood. The blankets in which we are wrapped, the colors in which we are dressed, the nursery in which we sleep, and the toys that help us learn all reinforce that we come as either a girl or a boy to take our place in the human family.[1]

Gender,[2] which is a social construction, is central to our identity, and each of us knows the embarrassment of not identifying another person's gender correctly. A casual comment about a "handsome" baby who turns out to be a girl is usually followed by an apology and some lame excuse about it "being hard to tell when there isn't much hair." Such mistakes are certainly less damaging when the child is very young.

Recently I read a story that described an eight-year-old girl who had suffered extensive burns in a camping accident. Eating in a restaurant with her parents, she overheard a curious person at a nearby table describe her as a "disfigured little boy." The comment about her scars did not hurt as much, she told her parents, as the observer's mistake about her gender. She wanted everyone to know that she's a *girl.*

What does it mean to experience life as a male or a female human being? One of the key issues of our day is the matter of gender differentiation.[3] We cannot help but be interested in this topic, for it so directly affects our self-understanding. Many questions will claim our attention in this study. What does God purpose by creating humanity with this chief distinctive? Why has there been a "battle of the sexes" throughout much of human history? What is unique to being male? What is unique to being female? How are we alike, and how are we different? In this chapter, I engage these important clues to our identity as a man or a woman who together share the journey of becoming human.

Biblical Perspectives

The creation accounts tell us that God made human beings as male and female, both bearing God's own image (Gen 1:27). Gender identity was not an afterthought or the result of human sinning, as some early Greeks imagined. Our human sexuality as female and male is a good gift from God, for which we should be grateful. Only human beings are given the specific reference of being male and female, rather than "according to their kind."

Genesis 2 offers the perceptive insight that we were created as sexual beings for wholeness. No companionship was found among the animals for the creature that God had formed out of the ground, hence the need for one who truly corresponds, yet is different. God's own wisdom is reflected in the words of the ancient writer: "It is not good that the man should be alone" (Gen 2:18). The intimate connection between the woman and the man is depicted in the beautiful narrative that describes the woman as being "built up from a rib out of Adam's side." Unlike the man, she was not taken from the ground, but from his own body. Phyllis Trible describes the significance of this action: "Built of raw material from the earth creature, rather than from the earth, the woman is unique in creation."[4] Thus, man and woman are of one flesh, made for one another, each partner revealing the other's uniqueness.

God played matchmaker in this passage, bringing the woman to the man. Obviously, this creature far surpassed what God had brought to Adam for naming. The delight that Adam expressed when he first encountered Eve was rapturous. "This at last is bone of my bones and flesh of my flesh," he exulted. When he met Eve, he knew better who he was. Evidently Adam had no awareness of his maleness until he met his counterpart, although he was aware of his loneliness and incompleteness. He made a little pun (we have to be able to read Hebrew to get his joke) acknowledging their unity and distinctiveness: "This shall be called woman (*ishshah*) because from man (*ish*) was taken this" (Gen 2:23).

Traditionalist interpreters have often read their own views of the male and female relationship into the passage, insisting that the woman was secondary and, therefore, to be under Adam's authority.[5] We should not conclude, however, that somehow woman is inferior because this story places her creation after that of the man. One could as easily argue that Adam was a "rough draft" and God decided, "I can do better than that!" Actually, the creation of humanity is not complete until there is male and female. The biblical writer's point is that women and men form the basic unit of the human family and, as male and female human beings, express the wholeness of humanity.

The word "helper" or "helpmeet" (Gen 2:18) is used in the older translations to refer to the woman; however, we should remember that God is often described as "helper" in the Old Testament (Exod 18:4; Ps 33:20). Thus, rather than being a term of subordination, "helper" means one suitable as co-creator and complementary partner. A better word, perhaps, is companion. Men and women will be companions throughout life.

The relationship between Adam and Eve, representing all men and women who will follow, is to be a mutual relationship that is full of respect and celebrates the diversity in unity. Peter Hodgson characterizes this relationship as "the primordial community in which human beings can be free for the other."[6] Even though marriage is God's idea and the most intimate of human relationships, we cannot view all of the meaning of human sexuality through the lens of marriage.[7] That is an opportunity provided by our sexuality as male and female, but we are related as male and female already.

God directed our human forebears to "be fruitful and multiply," and certainly procreation is one of the main reasons that, like the animals, we are created with biological complementarity as male and female. Unlike the animals, we are conscious of our sexuality and make choices about our relationships. When the Bible describes the union between wife and husband as "one flesh," this descriptive metaphor speaks not only of their physical and emotional intimacy, but of their offspring—children who embody the intermingled genetic codes of their parents. Of course, grandparents will claim their stunning contribution to the child's intelligence and strength of character! Creating a family through bearing children is an expression of commitment and hope. The loving context of the family provides the best environment for the nurture of daughters and sons.

According to the Bible, however, procreation is not the only purpose for human sexual intimacy. Rather, this form of sharing has both a celebrative and a unitive function. One of the most neglected and misinterpreted books in Holy Scripture is the Song of Songs. The early church fathers were so embarrassed about human sexuality that they thought of this love poem as an allegory of the relationship between Christ and the church—obviously they never pressed the details of the lyrics for precise meaning. There, right in the middle of the Old Testament, is an unblushing celebration of the goodness and unity of sexual intimacy between two young lovers. No Greek suspicion of the body is found here. (I would quote at length, but my editor might give me an "R" rating for this section.)

The Canticles offer a sensual portrayal of mutual enjoyment, without shame, showing God's graceful intention for the human sexual relationship. Phyllis Trible, distinguished Old Testament scholar, has suggested that these chapters redeem the "love story gone awry" of Genesis 2 and 3.[8] Unlike the experience of Adam and Eve who felt shame and hid their nakedness because of their sin, this couple celebrated without inhibition the erotic pleasures of touch, smell, taste, beauty, and shared solitude. The Bible shows a much healthier attitude toward human sexual expressions than what has developed in Christian tradition.[9]

The Shattering Effect of Sin

The friendship and interdependence between the woman and the man is shattered by human sin. One of the clearest expressions of their alienation from God is their alienation from one another. Deception, prostitution, incest, rape, and divorce stain the pages of scripture, pointing to sin's destructive power in human relationships. Created for intimate communion, the man and the woman now become suspicious of one another, not quite able to trust the other who is "different." The woman and the man have become sexes in opposition.

Historically, women have been blamed for the sinfulness of human persons—"After all, didn't she eat of the apple first?" This belief has been used to justify all sorts of measures to keep women "in their place" because they might cause something even worse to happen. The church fathers waxed long on the perversity of Eve, that "seductive siren, source of sin," and wrote that women were forced to carry the stigma of being the "corrupter of Eden" and the "devil's gateway."[10] The Protestant reformers were not much kinder, as we see from Martin Luther's stark accusation in his *Table Talk*:

> God created Adam Master and Lord of living creatures, but Eve spoilt it all when she persuaded him to set himself above God's will. 'Tis you women, with your tricks and artifices, that lead men into error.

Thus, a malignant image of women has colored much of the church's theology of sexuality.[11]

The subordination of women, however, is a result of human fallenness. It is not God's divinely ordained pattern for relating. Sin brings with it the curse of struggle in the marital relationship and a loss of mutuality characterized by the husband "ruling" (Gen 3:16). This ruling was translated into social and religious customs that granted to men wide-ranging privileges that were denied to women.

In Hebrew culture a woman left her family at marriage, bringing the necessary dowry, and was considered her husband's possession. Property rights, official standing in the worshiping community, laws of inheritance, and unfair divorce laws all reinforced the male-centered culture in which they lived.[12] The effects of the primal disruption caused by sin are seen throughout the biblical material as well as human history. That women have been treated as the "second sex" is well documented and is currently being challenged in many societies.[13]

A continuing problem for biblical interpreters has been to understand that much of scripture reflects "making the best of paradise lost." From the passages that reflect the alienation and broken relationships of sinful humanity, we have drawn conclusions about the "nature" of man or the "nature" of woman. These texts that reflect male domination are not God's ideal for human relationships, but show the enduring effects of human sinfulness.

We often overlook the fact that men have suffered greatly, as well, in the disorientation caused by sin. Work became a burden, and the intimacy Adam enjoyed with the earth was broken. Tilling and serving the ground, which should have been a joyful exercise, resulted in thorns and thistles; and with difficulty, a living has been coaxed from the ground (Gen 3:18-19). Modern men often suffer alienation from their families because of the burden of work.

Shared Work

God gave two responsibilities to the human beings: procreation and dominion. The text does not differentiate between the sexes in assigning this work. Actually the Bible is quite flexible about what comprises "men's work" and "women's work," except for the obvious: women will be mothers, and men will be fathers. The work of men and women does not divide into the public and private spheres, as some have suggested.[14] Both worked in a variety of ways tending flocks, gleaning in the fields, instructing the children, and caring for the extended family.

The Bible offers some surprising glimpses of the work patterns of women in the Ancient Near East and the first century Mediterranean world. The industrious woman who received praise in Proverbs 31 was hardly confined to the home! Priscilla and Aquila were the original "two-career couple," sharing the vocation of tent-making and serving as itinerant missionaries. Lydia, entrepreneur and head of her household, sounded positively modern (Acts 16). She probably had earned an M.B.A. that the text just fails to mention.

Men and women are called to build good homes together, but our sharing goes beyond procreative and domestic purposes. The particular contributions of men and women are needed to build good societies, also. We need both women and men in government, education, business, and ministry. Harmonious cooperation between the sexes is necessary for the common good, and a more balanced perspective is possible when shaped by the insights of both. The violence of a male-dominated social policy has brought us to the brink of ecological disaster; we desperately need to have the voices of women included that together we might preserve our earth and our species.[15]

Marriage is not the only relationship between men and women, and I would not want us to conclude that an unmarried person is less than complete. At points in all of our lives, we are single— through death, divorce, or the fact that we never married.

Yet we remain fundamentally related as humans who are either male or female, who need one another to become whole as human beings. Our lives are given structure and uniqueness through the many relationships we share as distinctive members of one humanity.

In the seminary where I taught for eleven years, I was the only female member of my department. My relationship to my four male colleagues was one of mutual respect and collaboration. I was challenged by their experience in teaching and their interactions with students. We brought different styles to the classroom and, often, accented different issues in our courses. The students in our school were enriched by viewing these collegial relationships, and we offered greater breadth in our subject area because of them.

All persons, whether married or unmarried, are in relationship as male and female because that is how we are created. That both women and men bear the image of God tells us something about equal human dignity and the one who is our creator. Part of our shared work is to reflect the character of God on the earth. Neither male nor female can do this alone, but we can as interdependent creatures of God. As we live in a community forged out of equal but different beings, we reflect the inner richness of God's own life, who dwells eternally as Trinity.[16]

Thus, when we speak about God, we should use language that reflects this diversity. The Bible is careful to speak of God in this way, describing the deity with feminine and maternal images (Hos 11:1; Deut 32:18; Isa 66:12-13) as well as masculine and paternal images (Ps 103:13; Exod 15:3; Hos 2:16). Scripture does not portray God in exclusively masculine symbols, nor exclusively feminine symbols, but in images that tell us of the motherly and fatherly character of God.[17] Yet we must remember that no human images can fully describe God, the One who transcends the duality of gender as we humans experience it.

Although the husband and wife form the basic family structure in the Bible, there are other expressions of family as well. Polygamy was commonly practiced from the time of the early patriarchs until the time of the Israelite kings. There was the widowed Naomi and her widowed daughter-in-law, Ruth, who clung to each other for survival in a patriarchal culture. Hosea was a single father—most of the time—caring for the children alone (Hos 1-3). Two sisters and their brother—Mary, Martha, and Lazarus—constituted a household in Bethany, a place of welcome hospitality for Jesus (Luke 10:38-42).

The Bible freely acknowledges that not all persons will live in an enduring marriage relationship. While affirming the appropriateness of marriage for many, Jesus also described persons who should not marry: "because they were born so, or were made so by other persons, or have renounced marriage for the sake of the kingdom of heaven" (Matt 19:12 RSV). Singleness falls within God's purpose, as does marriage.

Beyond the Curse

The plight of women drew forth Jesus' compassion on more than one occasion. He directly challenged the divorce laws that were concessions for the "hardness of heart . . . but from the beginning it was not so" (Matt 18:8-9), which suggests that such inequality was a result of human sin, not really God's intention at all. A divorced or widowed woman was left with little resources for survival in her culture, and Jesus challenged the structure that oppressed her. The persistent widow was a heroine in one of Jesus' parables because she did not lose heart (Luke 18:1-8).

More than his pronouncements about women, Jesus' actions toward them marked him as one who received his human sisters as equals.[18] His attitude contrasted sharply with the rabbis who considered the woman as an inferior being, a detriment to her husband's spirituality, and incapable of religious devotion herself. His friendship with the two sisters of Bethany, Mary and Martha, is a prominent part of the Gospel of John(11:144; 12:1-8).When confronted with the woman "taken in adultery," Jesus allowed her no more condemnation for her sin than that of the men who dragged her into his presence (John 8). His response to her was very different from the double standard of morality found in the Old Testament, where a woman was much more severely punished for sexual transgressions (Gen 38:24) and considered "unclean" simply because of her menstrual flow (Lev 11–16). Shielding her from further embarrassment and granting her forgiveness, Jesus restored her human dignity through challenging her to a new way of life (John 8:11).

Jesus welcomed the discipleship of women. He believed they were capable of understanding his message about the inbreaking rule of God and of following him in the radical obedience of faith. Although he selected for symbolic and pragmatic purposes twelve men as his core group, women were included as faithful disciples in the Gospel accounts (Luke 8:2-3).[19] Further, as is often recounted, all four Gospels tell us that Jesus entrusted the news of the resurrection to the women who had come to anoint his body and were blessed to encounter him as the risen one (Matt 28:9; Mark 16:9-11; Luke 24:6-9; John 20:11-18).

One of the more enigmatic sayings of Jesus that related to human sexuality was his response to the Sadducees, "For when they rise from the dead, they neither marry nor are given in marriage, but are like angels in heaven" (Mark 12:25). As you might imagine, this passage has created much anxiety on the part of persons who have been preceded in death by their spouses. Did Jesus suggest that all distinction between male and female will disappear in the world to come and that our significant relationships will cease?

Jesus certainly did not mean that we would grow wings or that our gender would disappear in the world to come. Sexuality as male or female is not an expendable part of our identity, contrary to what Augustine thought. The question of the Sadducees was about establishing progeny for seven brothers, each of whom had married the same woman. In their eyes, it was important that a man continue the holy genealogies of Israel, and none of the brothers had fathered children. Further, they were really trying to trick Jesus into saying something about the resurrection that they might condemn him.

In the age to come, marriage and procreation will cease; these are responsibilities only for our present historical lives. (Parents of teenagers will surely give thanks.) Jesus did not mean that we will not have enduring relationships of significance with those with whom we have shared our lives.

Paul shared Jesus' perspective on marriage as a temporal relationship, a part of this world order (I Cor 7:25-35). Like Jesus, the apostle had a positive view of human sexuality. Paul expressed the interdependence of woman and man when he wrote,

> In the Lord woman is not independent of man or man independent of woman. For just as woman came from man, so man comes through woman; but all things come from God. (I Cor 11:11-12)

The key to this passage and to Paul's thinking was his affirmation of the equality of women and men. In fact, women had such prominent roles in the early churches that the synagogues and other religious groups were scandalized. Jesus' egalitarian treatment of women left its stamp on his followers, though they struggled to conform to his vision of the rule of God, where gender and status no longer can bar membership.[20]

Unity in Diversity

"Why can't a woman be more like a man?" asked Professor Henry Higgins in the musical *My Fair Lady*. The pompous professor did not know that he was more like a woman than he knew. Men and women share many characteristics, and thus it is difficult to say precisely how men and women differ. For instance, talking about human virtues is much easier than discussing male or female virtues. Professor Higgins had the mistaken idea that one of the sexes, the male, was normative and thus was to be the measure of the other. That is hardly the best approach to understanding the meaning of gender or for keeping the peace!

Our understanding of gender differences is often limited to the biological differences that allow reproduction. Our sexuality, however, is a comprehensive way of being a human being. Not only does our socialization differ, but our way of being in the world, relating to God and others, is substantially influenced by whether we are female or male. Of course, we are all aware of stereotypes attached to our specific gender, but these are often more socially conditioned than innate, and we need not rehearse them here.

When we compare women and men, it is important to remember that "different" does not mean better or worse. That would be like saying an apple is better than an orange or entering into a conversation worthy of Dennis and Margaret or Susie and Calvin, of comic strip fame. Men and women are actually more alike than we are different, yet there are differences. Our biological inheritance as well as our social context make these possible.

Currently, some very interesting and complex research is being conducted on the possible difference in the brain organization of men and women. Despite a huge overlap, these studies suggest that the reason boys seem to excel in math and spatial visualization and girls lead in verbal facility and intricate finger and hand movements—to mention the most distinctive features—is because their brains function in different ways. Apparently men and women employ the two hemispheres of their brains in distinctive strategies. Even when attempting identical tasks and coming up with the same results, evidence suggests that women and men may be working with different parts of the brain. Whether this difference is strictly biological or is affected by playing with Lincoln logs rather than dolls (with whom one must, of course, converse) is an open question.

Ruth Hubbard, a retired Harvard biologist, has written extensively in this area and concludes that in most societies men and women live very different lives, and so we develop very different capabilities. We do not know how to translate anatomical sex differences into behavioral difference. Therefore, we should avoid generalizations about how men and women should function. Arguments from earlier days about women lacking leadership ability and men lacking nurturing ability are simply false. The traditional roles that men and women have played in society have often reinforced such myths, but there is currently a significant degree of awareness of how damaging these have been to both sexes.[21]

What does it mean to be feminine, and what does it mean to be masculine? Traits thought to define masculinity include being rational, athletic, aggressive, and unemotional. Those more often associated with femininity include being intuitive, nurturing, dependent, and emotional. This is an unfair polarization and reflects a great deal of inequality and pressure toward conformity. It is not surprising that our society values these so-called "masculine" characteristics more than the feminine ones, given the prominence men retain in our culture. We must remember, however, that not until the nineteenth century was "home-making" viewed as a full-time occupation, and it has been buttressed by stressing the exclusive emotional suitability of women for that role.[22]

Rigid stereotypes are breaking apart, however, and we are seeing new freedom for individual women and men to express their human gifts in a variety of ways, even if they run counter to prevailing expectations. Men are learning that they have wonderful capacities for tenderness and vulnerability that are distinctively masculine, and women are learning that they can be strong, logical, and assertive without sacrificing their femininity. Any husband who has coached his wife through delivery no longer believes she is "the weaker sex."

Further, we see changes in vocational direction as students experience greater freedom of choice in following their abilities. Daddy no longer gasps when his little girl wants to be an astronaut. We are aware that we are living in a time of intense reflection about what constitutes sex-appropriate behavior. Clothing, hair-styles, and professional opportunities are merging in unprecedented ways, and many of us are trying to catch up with the implications of such sweeping changes.

The "women's movement" beginning in the sixties has had a wide-ranging impact on American society. Though some have feared anything related to "feminism," many persons acknowledge that gains both for men and women have resulted.[23] Equal pay and opportunity are slowly becoming a cornerstone in our places of work, which is "justice for all."

This movement is not suggesting that women and men can simply exchange roles or that no gender differences will remain. We would be quite impoverished if men and women were not complementary. One of our most enduring distinctives is that women tend to value relational connections with other people, while men accent the significance of individualism. Both genders can benefit by consciously seeking a blend of these two dimensions. One of the results could be that men might live longer. On the average, men die about seven years younger than women, in large measure because of the pressure toward achievement, winning, and remaining in control. Another result of a blend between community and individualism could be a reduction of the incidence of depression in women, which is considerably more frequent than for men. A lack of the sense of a worthy self plagues many women who sacrifice themselves for the good of others.

To be a healthy society, we must value the contributions of both women and men. Individuals need to be encouraged to celebrate the uniqueness of gender, especially in a day that is characterized by a great deal of confusion about maleness and femaleness. Our kids are enthralled by videos that are filled with the icons of popular culture, often persons without clear gender identity. The androgynous blurring of the sexes, or "gender-bending" as some call it, provides little assistance for adolescents who are trying to figure out who they are. They receive conflicting information about what is expected of them and how they can succeed.

The early messages parents offer to children about how they are equally valued, whether boy or girl, are very important. Parents and childcare workers can slow down culture's intense pressure toward role conformity by the activities they encourage the children to pursue and by what tasks they perform in the home. A professional couple I know shares all the domestic jobs except one: the husband does all of the cooking. When this couple's daughter was younger, she would often question the presence of the mother in the kitchen at her friends' homes. "I didn't know women could do that," she exclaimed. Now a teenager, she has been raised without rigid expectations about "men's work" and "women's work."

Several years ago I served as a pastor in rural Kentucky. This arrangement worked very well, and the church began to grow a little. In fact, the people were quite proud of themselves for being rather progressive. We had not counted on one of the results, however. Whenever the children would leave the main service of worship for their own session, they often liked to "play church," setting up a pulpit, holding mock baptisms with dolls, and conducting fellowship suppers. It seems that the little girls would never let the little boys have the coveted role of playing "preacher." The children's worker would patiently explain, "Now girls, little boys can be preachers, too." But the bossy girls weren't too convinced, for I was the only preacher that they had known.

We tend to believe something is possible once we have experienced it personally. Children, adolescents, and even adults can be encouraged to put aside narrow definitions of masculinity and femininity when they encounter, first hand, persons engaged in nontraditional vocational roles. Overcoming years of conditioning is difficult, but we can experience a great deal of personal freedom and a new appreciation for the diversity of human gifts shared by men and women.

I recently sat by an older gentleman on a lengthy airplane flight. As he was boarding the plane, he caught a glimpse in the cockpit that a young woman would be serving as one of the pilots. He spluttered all the way back to his seat about women trying to do "what they had no business doing." I was not too anxious to open a conversation with him, fearing he might ask what I did professionally. He was on his way to visit his granddaughter, a research chemist in a major university. Sensing how proud he was of her, I asked him some questions about the obstacles she had faced in completing her schooling and gaining this highly competitive position. He spoke with disdain about professors who devoted more of their time to her male student colleagues, thinking they had more commitment and future in the area. "It's been tough, but she didn't give up," he explained. As I gave him what I hoped was a knowing look, he grinned about his earlier protests concerning one of the pilots who now had us well on our way in the air.

God has gifted the human family with the duality of sexes, neither of which is to be prized over the other. The gender of each person is to be affirmed as the unique way each of us will function in the world. Our bodies are to be treasured as marvelous creations of God that we can enjoy fully as the means by which we communicate, establish intimacy, and serve others. Because we are embodied selves, our physical actions must be tempered with respect for others and ourselves. We must teach one another through the home and the community of faith a deeper ethical sensitivity about the proper stewardship of our sexuality.[24] Indeed, as Christians we are called to make holy covenants of fidelity and hope that can sustain our living and stand against much of the exploitation of our culture.

Perhaps persons of faith face no greater challenge today than a new appreciation of our sexuality. Centuries of male domination and anti-sexual theology are finally ebbing, which is good news. It is an exciting time to be a human being; may we learn to celebrate the wonder of humanity as male and female.

Endnotes

[1]Occasionally, persons are born without clear assignation. Medical intervention must ensue.

[2]Gerda Lerner, *The Creation of Patriarchy* (New York: Oxford University Press, 1986) 238, distinguishes "gender" from "sex." She defines gender as "the cultural definition of behavior defined as appropriate to the sexes in a given society at a given time."

[3]Specifically, Elizabeth Janeway, *Man's World, Woman's Place: A Study in Social Mythology* (New York: Morrow, 1971); Evelyn Fox Keller, *Reflections on Gender and Science* (New Haven CT: Yale University Press, 1985); and Luce Irigaray, *An Ethics of Sexual Differences*, trans. C. Burke and G. C. Gill (Ithaca NY: Cornell University Press, 1993).

[4]Phyllis Trible, *God and the Rhetoric of Sexuality* (Philadelphia: Fortress Press, 1978) 96.

[5]Specifically, John Piper and Wayne Grudem, eds. *Recovering Biblical Manhood and Womanhood: A Response to Evangelical Feminism* (Wheaton IL: Crossway Books, 1991).

[6]Peter Hodgson, *Winds of the Spirit: A Constructive Christian Theology* (Louisville KY: John Knox/Westminster, 1994) 179.

[7]The well-known Christian ethicist James B. Nelson argues that the sexual relations of homosexual as well as heterosexual persons "can richly express and be the vehicle of God's humanizing intentions." *Embodiment: An Approach to Sexuality and Christian Theology* (Minneapolis: Augsburg,1978) 197. See also John Boswell, *Christianity, Social Tolerance, and Homosexuality* (Chicago: University of Chicago Press, 1980).

[8]See Trible, 144-65.

[9]Margaret R. Miles, *Practicing Christianity: Critical Perspectives for an Embodied Spirituality* (New York: Crossroad, 1988) 99, offers useful insight in this regard: "Christian tradition, marked by 'the triumph of Augustine's treatment of sexuality' does not provide a way to see sexual relationship as a format for Christian growth." Rather, it portrays just the opposite, in the main.

[10]George H. Tavard, *Women in Christian Tradition* (Notre Dame IN: University of Notre Dame Press, 1993) especially 57-96, reviews the misogynistic perspectives promulgated by the Church Fathers.

[11]Other volumes providing a sampling of such messages are Elizabeth A. Clark, *Women in the Early Church* (Wilmington DE: Michael Glazier, Inc. 1983); Frances and Joseph Gies, *Women in the Middle Ages* (New York: Barnes and Noble, 1980); and Rosemary Radford Reuther, *Religion and Sexism* (New York: Simon and Schuster, 1974).

[12]Helpful for background material is Rachel Biale, *Women and Jewish Law: An Exploration of Women's Issues in Halakic Sources* (New York: Schocken Books, 1984). See also Athalya Brenner, *The Israelite Woman: Social Role and Literary Type in Biblical Narrative* (Sheffield: JSOT Press, 1985).

[13]A collection edited by Ursula A. King, *Feminist Theology from the Third World* (Maryknoll NY: Orbis, 1994) provides access to many disparate cultures.

[14]See the traditionalist essay of Elisabeth Elliot, "The Essence of Femininity," in *Recovering Biblical Manhood and Womanhood*, eds. John Piper and Wayne Grudem (Wheaton: Crossway Books, 1991) 394-99.

[15]Lisa Sowle Cahill, *Between the Sexes* (Philadelphia: Fortress Press, 1985) 92ff., warns that we not assign all nurturing and domestic roles to women, nor the public, economic and political roles to men.

[16]See Mary Timothy Prokes' fine study, *Mutuality: The Human Image of Trinitarian Love* (New York: Paulist Press, 1993).

[17]A constructive approach to this vexed question is offered by Brian Wren, *What Language Shall I Borrow?* (New York: Crossroad, 1989).

[18]Elisabeth Moltmann-Wendel, *The Women Around Jesus* (New York: Crossroad, 1982) 2-4.

[19]Susan Nelson Dunfee, *Beyond Servanthood: Christianity and the Liberation of Women* (Lanham MD: University Press of America, 1984) surveys how early Christianity empowered women with authority for liberative activity in the service of the Gospel.

[20]E. Schüssler Fiorenza maintains that the *basileia* vision of Jesus sought to overturn all patriarchal structures and create, instead, a discipleship of equals. See her tour de force, *In Memory of Her: A Feminist Theological Reconstruction of Christian Origins* (New York: Crossroad, 1983) 118-54.

[21]Mary McClintock Fulkerson, *Charging the Subject: Women's Discourses and Feminist Theology* (Minneapolis: Augsburg Fortress Press, 1994) argues against a contemporary bend in feminist theology that privileges woman's experience at some definable entity against male experience. Basing feminist theology on the criteria of women's experience not only denies the particularity of the experience of different women; it also tends to deny the shared human experience of men and women.

[22]Gerda Lerner, *The Creation of Feminist Consciousness* (Oxford: Oxford University Press, 1993) 34, argues that the sequestering of women in such private enterprises is a major assumption about gender in a patriarchal society.

[23]Many persons struggle with the compatibility of Christianity and feminism, due in part to the freight attached to the term. A helpful introduction for more "traditionalist" Christians has been written by Elaine Storkey, *What's Right with Feminism* (Grand Rapids MI: Eerdmans, 1985).

[24]I recommend Stanley Grenz, *Sexual Ethics: A Biblical Perspective* (Dallas: Word, Inc., 1990) as a timely introduction to Christian sexual ethics.

The Pursuits of Humanity: Culture and Community

America has just endured what some persons have described as a "decade of greed." We might recall Ivan Boesky's 1986 commencement address at the University of California Business School in Berkeley (before he went to jail) in which he declared: "Greed is healthy." In the film *Wall Street*, financial wizard Gordon Gekko offers a similar contribution. "Greed," he said, "for lack of a better word, is good. Greed is right. Greed works."

We are now observing in broken lives and a debt-ridden economy the results of an unbridled monetary quest "to get ahead." Tearful testimonies at trials remind us that persons are meant for pursuits other than simply making money. While this is a necessary and significant part of being human, our lives must include many other dimensions for us to be fully human. The New Testament verse, "What shall it profit persons to gain the whole world and lose their own lives?" reminds us of the devastating consequences of greed.

What role does work play in the formation of our character?[1] Is our work only to be endured—as many seem to think—so that it can support our leisure? Does technology assist us in becoming more fully human, or does it distance us from the earth and others?[2] What is the real purpose of people? Can our governments actually foster community? In this chapter I examine the pursuits of human beings in terms of culture and community and acknowledge that both of these are needed to nourish the wholeness of our humanity—which includes our spirituality.

From a Garden to a City

The biblical story begins with two persons in a garden and ends in a city filled with all the nations of the earth (Rev 21). This turn of events suggests that much is to occur between creation and consummation. God has created a world for which we must care and has granted considerable aptitudes to us that we must explore. Remarkably, scripture recounts the technological and cultural development of human beings without condemnation, except when humans sought to displace God, as the story of the tower of Babel illustrates.

The fourth chapter of Genesis intertwines family relations and the development of human culture.

> Adah bore Jubal; he was the ancestor of those who live in tents and have livestock. His brother's name was Jubal; he was the ancestor of all those who play the lyre and pipe. Zillah bore Tubal-Cain, who made all kinds of bronze and iron tools. The sister of Tubal-Cain was Naamah (20-22).

The narrative is quite matter of fact, as if these pursuits were the appropriate actions to take to fulfill God's command to have dominion. Diversity of gifts and interests and a constructive division of labor mark these activities of our forebears. Nomadic clans living close to the land, makers of plowshares and swords, and those who nourish the spirit with their music all contribute to the common good.

Creativity and Adaptation

Creativity and adaptation as well as the love of art and beauty show our kinship to the creator, who fills our world with inestimable artistry so that even the "heavens declare the glory of God" (Ps 19).[3] Those who crafted the tabernacle and the temple displayed their abilities in architecture with wood, cloth, and precious metals and stones. They acknowledged that God had "endowed with skill" (Exod 28:3) for these pursuits.[4]

We see development in international relations as Solomon collected the materials with which to build the temple. Hiram, the king of Tyre, thought it a privilege to provide the legendary cedars of Lebanon, which form the basic structure of the new house of worship (I Kgs 5:6). Perhaps because of these contacts the temple singers of Israel were well known in the ancient Near Eastern world; the collection of Psalms, complete with instructions for the instrumentalists, bears witness to the refined worship practices of the Hebrews. Their faith was nourished through these cultural expressions.

The occupation of the principal characters of the New Testament was important, for this was not an incidental part of their lives. We know that Jesus probably learned carpentry from Joseph, Matthew worked in government service, Peter ran a fishing fleet, Paul made tents, Lydia imported and sold purple cloth, Dorcas was a homemaker and a seamstress, and Cornelius served in the military service. These vocations were not a barrier to their faith, but became, for many of them, a channel through which they could express their devotion and witness to the power of Christ in their lives while being responsible members of the human community.

We must realize that we do not have to escape our world in order to be close to God.[5] Much in our heritage as Christians sees everything about the physical and material world as so corrupt that we must flee its clutches as best we can.[6] This perspective drove many of the early Christians toward a lifestyle that rejected basic bodily desires as sinful. Some of them lived in the desert, trying to escape all of the corrupting influences of human society, its sensuality in particular. During the time of the Reformation, the Swiss reformer, Ulrich Zwingli, felt that images and pictures should be removed from the church because they were a distraction to true worship, not an integral part.

But this is a one-sided reading of scripture. Karl Rahner, a significant Catholic theologian, encourages us to develop a faith that "loves the earth." He suggests that because we are embodied, physical beings, we can best encounter God through the world prepared for our dwelling. God meets us here—as is ultimately demonstrated by the "Word becoming flesh." Hence, the good things of this earth are not to be shunned, and it is appropriate to celebrate the varied expressions of human creativity and adaptation that we see in the arts and technology. These are not the highest good, for only God deserves that description, according to Jesus. But our human creativity does point beyond us to our maker, the living God.

Governing Structures

The development of technological skills was accompanied by new structures to govern and regulate human social relations. The Israelites demanded that a monarchy replace the loose confederacy of tribes and regional judges they had known during the period of the Exodus and the settlement in the land of promise. Perceiving their status as a nation to be weak and unable to compete with the more powerful nations around them, they persuaded the priest Samuel to anoint a king who might defend them from their enemies.[7] The Old Testament interprets their request as the people's rejection of God as their sovereign leader (I Sam 8:7).

Perhaps we see the beginning of tension between the demands of God and the state upon human persons. The Old Testament ironically celebrates the time of David as the model kingship, but it has little praise for the other kings and queens who, after the time of Solomon, ruled over a divided nation.

The tragedies of Israel's period of exile are well known. Periods of deportation were followed by extended times of foreign domination. During the time of Jesus, Israel was little more than a vassal state, partitioned into three regions that had a Roman appointed puppet government. An occupation army plagued the people of the land, and at least one group of priests attempted to find ways to work in collaboration with their oppressors. Critics of Jesus attempted to press him into commenting on this uneasy relationship with Rome.[8]

"Render unto Caesar what is Caesar's and to God what is God's," may be some of the best known words of Jesus. He acknowledged that two powers compete for human loyalty and that we are subject to both. Therefore, he urged that we learn to balance these responsibilities in a constructive manner, and he set an example for us by paying his taxes. (I have often wished I could use his method, that is, pulling in a fish, around April 15!)

The difficulty comes, of course, when the posture of the state attempts to supersede the rule of God in our lives. The Royalists imprisoned John Bunyan, the author of *Pilgrim's Progress*, in the Bedford jail for twelve years for his activities as a preacher. William Penn suffered greatly because of an unholy alliance between the church and the state. His resistance to the teaching of the state church forced him to withdraw from Oxford. Seeing clearly the need for religious toleration, he devoted his life to founding a colony in America that would insure liberty of conscience for Quakers and others.

At times, the state has offered protection to those abused by ecclesiastical authorities, such as Frederick the Wise's care of Martin Luther.[9] He had his soldiers whisk Luther away when his life was in jeopardy from the powers of Rome. In our day, the government of India, for example, seeks to protect those religious minorities who suffer violence and the threat of displacement from the majority religious body.

Utopian Dreams of Humanity

Every society has dreamed of establishing the perfect community, a utopia in which all live in cooperation. In such a society, the work of all would be interdependent and valued; personal freedom would be in proper balance with concern for the common good

Over the centuries a number of experimental communities have been created for that purpose.[10]

In New Harmony, Indiana, on the banks of the Wabash River George Rapp founded such a community in 1814. Artisans, philosophers, farmers, and others came together to offer their particular contributions to a new society. The Harmony Society, also called the Rappites, though eccentric in many of their beliefs, applauded art and science as significant religious expressions. In addition to their unique practices of worship, they were engaged in actions toward social justice and, like the Shakers[11]—another utopian experiment—took in persons who were homeless and without family support. Enforced celibacy and an insular existence in the larger society led to the demise of both of these sects, yet they sought to blend culture and community in an enriching way.

The Marxist vision is a more secular version of the utopian dream.[12] The significance of work occupies the center of the stage in the human theatre of history, according to this understanding. Marx sought to lay the theoretical groundwork for a society in which a person could work without suffering exploitation. He envisioned a form of communal sharing that would replace a capitalist society with its wealthy elite. Recent changes in the intellectual and territorial map of Europe and Asia demonstrate both the force and futility of many aspects of this social experiment, although the Marxist influence continues.

Work as Service and Self-Expression

Contemporary theologians reflect on the phenomenon that modern people are less concerned about guilt than with meaninglessness.[13] I believe they are saying something very important about our culture and the lack of attention that has been given by our churches to the meaning of our work, one of the "worldly concerns"—as the frontier preachers called them. The role of work in our lives has been diminished through depersonalization and exaggerated economic expectations.

We hear of persons looking forward to retiring by age forty or fifty (sometimes even younger) to escape "the rat race." This goal serves ostensibly to justify hard driving years of impossible schedules that sacrifice health and meaningful family relationships to earn a certain economic level. Work is a means to an end in this scheme, not a channel for self-expression and service to others.

We have lost the sensitivity to work as "calling" that characterized even our grandparents. Even though persons might have lacked the same range of choices that persons today have, there was an accent on "honorable work."

My grandfather was a clock builder. From beautiful oak or cherry or ash, he would fashion the wooden case for grandfather clocks. He lost his sight in his earlier years, so he found ways to adapt his use of his carpentry tools. The one thing he could not do was install the actual clockworks—another man in his little town in Arkansas would do that final task. They shared a love of rich, hand-smoothed wood, and the deep chiming tones of these clocks. Their obvious pride in their work was matched by orders too numerous to fill. The simplicity and beauty of these clocks encouraged others in their area to value the work of their hands.

Wendell Berry, a poet and farmer in Port Royal, Kentucky, composed a collection of essays in which he insists that work without pleasure eventually leads both to a life without satisfaction and a deadening alienation from the land itself. He writes,

> More and more, we take for granted that work must be destitute of pleasure. More and more, we assume that if we want to be pleased we must wait until evening, or the weekend, or vacation, or retirement....Where is our comfort but in the free, uninvolved, finally mysterious beauty and grace of this world that we did not make, that has no price? Where is our pleasure but in working and resting kindly in the presence of this world?[14]

God did not give work as a curse to us.[15] Human beings were working prior to the alienating activities of their sin. The curse of our sinfulness is that it tends to diminish everything we attempt as human persons. Thus, our work becomes a meaningless burden rather than an expression of our unique identity. Whether it be teaching a class, painting a window, plowing a field, singing an aria, or directing traffic, work is a manifestation of our human nature and can be enriching and satisfying. We understand ourselves by the things that we make and the activities we pursue. We experience ourselves as creative and imaginative individuals through our work. Pleasure and a feeling of accomplishment nurture our sense of worth as human persons.

Persons whose whole identity is wrapped up in their work may feel worthless when that work is threatened. As I recently lost the job I have so dearly loved, I experienced a considerable measure of anxiety wondering who I am now that I am no longer a professor of theology at Southern Seminary in Louisville, Kentucky. This process of personal reflection has been healthful for me in that it has reminded me that our vocations as God's partners in this world transcend the particular location or job description. Further, I am learning about the danger of idolatry in clinging too tightly to an esteemed position.

Technology: Uses and Abuses

Do you remember some of the television commercials of the late fifties and early sixties? Riding the wave of early success in new forms of communication, these commercials made outlandish promises about a greatly reduced work load, especially for the American homemaker. Domestic robots who could serve as butler, maid, chef, and babysitter were especially tempting. Many of technology's promises have come to pass and, in many ways, work in the home, office, or place of business is made less strenuous. But is life any simpler? I chuckled when I read that the average homemaker actually spends more time doing laundry, cooking, and cleaning in our day than before the onslaught of "time-saving devices."

The computer and telecommunication revolution has offered more accessible information than we could imagine even a decade ago, but at what price? The rapidity of change and nearly instantaneous global news may contribute less to constructive responses than to a feeling of overwhelming paralysis. Technology that was meant to serve us seems, at times, to tyrannize us. Who among us has not battled with a "computer error" in billing? A convenient scapegoat for human error and a means of putting distance between merchant and client, the computer rules contemporary business, social services and, increasingly, education.

I am biting the hand that feeds me, of course, by drafting the above paragraph on my word processor! I certainly know the benefits of saying goodbye to manual typewriters and carbon paper, yet I am concerned that technology may have diminished the significance of work while, at the same time, contributing to an enormous ecological problem.[16]

How can technology diminish the meaning of our work? One writer suggests that mechanization and assembly-line methods of production make the individual more expendable than ever. If a person retires or dies, plenty of others can step right in and do essentially the same job. While we might applaud the team concept where persons can swap jobs to prevent boredom and promote good work relationships, this easy substitution means that no one person is indispensable. Life does go on even when one person no longer keeps step. We know that often a worker experiences great sadness when that person looks back over his or her life at retirement.[17] What did he or she really accomplish? "Will I be missed?" is a recurring thought.

Perhaps one of the reasons that our culture reveres artists, conductors, and writers is that their gifts set them apart as persons with unique contributions to make. Two very gifted American composers and conductors, Leonard Bernstein and Aaron Copeland, have died in recent years. Articles, eulogies, and memorial concerts have expressed our profound sense of national loss. We realize that they are really not replaceable, even though other gifted artists will follow.

This past summer I visited a display of Appalachian crafts near Asheville, North Carolina. Hand-hewn rockers, quilts with intricate regional patterns, and iron fireplace tools forged in the blacksmith's shop bore mute testimony to the value of work in the lives of their creators. As I strolled through the exhibit, I overheard appreciative comments about how well-made each craft was. These painstaking expressions of skill served not only to remind me of simpler times, but of the grace of creativity. It is well for each of us to cultivate the ability to make useful things for our homes and friends, for this can connect us in a meaningful way to work.

Obviously, not all of us are artists or skilled craftspersons Many of us work in jobs that have repetitious or menial aspects to them. We will have to learn ways to value our work and take pride in it, especially when it lacks the distinction of other forms of work. Our faithfulness and dependability can bring honor to even the most mundane form of occupation, especially when we welcome the dimensions of social relatedness inherent in most positions.

Technology not only has contributed to the loss of meaningful work for many, but its abuse is leading to a society on the brink of ecological disaster. In addition to an embarrassingly serious garbage disposal problem, daily we are polluting the only earth we have. Factories belch industrial wastes into our lakes and streams; scores of scientists devote their energies to weaponry; and oil spills darken the surrounding water and beaches, making them unfit for habitation or enjoyment. The very technology that allows mass production, nuclear energy, commerce, and material affluence threatens the life of our planet—which includes our existence as humans.

As long as greed dictates the use of technology, I fear there will be little regard for ecological preservation or for the cost to human lives. Many persons work in unsafe conditions and are forced to take early retirement because of the long-term harmful effects of their workplaces. Although the specific technology has grown more sophisticated, proper safeguards have often not kept pace. Protecting the company's profit rather than its employees seems to be the chief goal of some corporate leaders.

Although our lives are easier in many respects because of the technological advances of recent decades, we should be wary of the accompanying side effects. Mobile telephones, for example, tether us to work and prevent recreative solitude. Automobiles allow us great freedom in travel, yet fill the air with noxious fumes. Television has a numbing effect even as it allows us to be in greater touch with our world. In our relentless pursuit of developing and using technology, we must find a way to balance its benefits with its potential harm.[18]

The Creation of Community

One of the chief emphases of our study of what it means to be human is the necessity of living in community. As we have noted, humans function best in the community of collaboration and interdependence. True community respects individual uniqueness and affirms the unity of our shared humanity. Community is not simply a spiritual reality, although it certainly includes that dimension. Community provides the best context for vocation, as Martin Luther wisely knew: "We serve God, we love God, we serve and love our neighbors *in commune per vocatione*—in community through vocation."

A commonly ignored, but essential aspect of community is economic justice. The Old Testament provides several specific instructions on this matter. According to the law books,

• The earth is the Lord's (Lev 25:23). We are stewards and colonists and do not have permanent claim to any of the earth's goods.

- A tenant may not sell land, since every fifty years, in the year of jubilee, land reverts to its original holder or descendants (Lev 25:18).
- The fruits of the earth are subject to the tithe, of which one part goes to the tribe of Levi, which has no possession, "except for the Lord" (Deut 10:9).
- Another part of the tithe goes to the poor. The corners of the fields are to be left for the gleaners. Feasts are arranged to which widows, orphans, and the poor are invited (Deut 16).
- Every seven years is a sabbatical year. (Professors especially like this part of the biblical legislation.) The land is allowed to rest, and all may reap what it might put forth (Exod 23:11).
- An employer must pay the laborers their wages before sundown on the same day they earned them (Deut 24:14).
- An interest-free loan for the poor was compulsory because those with resources were to care for those in need (Deut 15:4-11).
- The poor could take the possessions of others in order to keep from starving (Deut 23:24-25).

These regulations were to prevent a few people from controlling all of the wealth while others lived in abject poverty. Jesus' own ministry reflected his faithfulness to this tradition.[19]

At times governments have sought to implement the biblical regulations, but usually have concluded that it "isn't really practical." Our world would be a better place, however, if these guidelines were followed consistently. Do you remember the central figure of Victor Hugo's *Les Miserables?* Jean Valjean was sent to prison for stealing bread to feed the hungry. He bitterly resented the merciless law that held him captive for fourteen years and haunted him for the rest of his life. The law violated the Bible's compassion for the poor.[20]

In addition to economic justice, community requires that persons be willing to acknowledge their need of others. Often this takes the form of emotional support, which requires that we be honest about our hurts and fears. The church where I make my spiritual home provides this kind of sustaining community. One Sunday as I looked around the congregation from my usual pew, I thought about the many hard things we have helped one another to bear in the past few years.

To my right sat a family whose eleven-year-old daughter was killed in a car accident earlier in the year. Two rows behind that family a grandmother was silently weeping: Christmas music always makes her think of her grandson who died at this time of year. In the choir was a young seminary student who just last year stood at the casket of his wife of four years. Sadly, I could mention many more. All of those persons were gathered for worship with those who have walked with them through their dark nights of the soul. Through their faith in God and the faithfulness of these Christian sisters and brothers, they are living with courage and hope in the midst of a caring community. This kind of community can only be created by God and sustained by the spirit of God.[21]

"Community" is a popular word these days. Political speeches refer to the desire to live in safe communities. College orientation sessions talk about creating a learning community comprised of diverse individuals. Real estate agents point out the advantages of a certain community. Each of these uses of community point to a dimension of cooperative human living. Authentic community does not obliterate diversity, but values its rich contribution. While it must chiefly attend to the common good, it does not trample individual interests underfoot. Set forth as an ideal, the actual building of community is an elusive, often frustrating goal, for we never achieve it perfectly "for here we have no lasting city, but we are looking for the city that is to come" (Heb 13:14).

Yet, the Bible maintains the vision of humans living in community with nature, God, and other human persons. Saint Augustine spoke of our eternal dwelling as the "city of God," citing a verse from Hebrews 13. Here, in faint outline, we see something of our true destiny and realize why the creation of community will only be complete in the future.[22]

The Book of Revelation, especially chapter 21, gives us a fuller picture of living in the community intended by God. In the "holy city," persons will enjoy a close relationship with God, for God "will dwell with them" (21:3). All the people will experience the comfort of God, and those things that trouble us—death, mourning, crying, and pain—will be no more. God will dry our tears and receive our continuous worship.[23]

Further, the city will reflect the glory of all nations of the earth. The real "united nations" will, at long last, be a reality. A place of beauty and purity, this eternal dwelling will also extend hospitality to the downtrodden of the world. The water of life is the gift promised to all who desire it (22:16), and only those who prefer falsehood will be excluded from the shalom of God.

The people of God will live eternally in the peace promised by Christ, a peace different from what the world gives. We are called to "wage peace" now in anticipation of our final dwelling. Because the Spirit of the Risen Lord already lives in our midst, we are encouraged to invest our lives toward building caring communities that can nurture wholeness. Our involvement in our churches and the social services of our towns and cities are important ways we can help establish peace.

Pursuing Culture and Community

I am writing this part of our reflection on what it means to be human during the Advent season. Insistent phone calls, letters soliciting funds, special offerings at church, and television commercials all remind us of the vast needs of people living within our same geographical area. At Christmas, the human spirit reaches toward those whose economic situation prevents celebrating the season of giving. These generous, unselfish efforts remind us that our lives should be devoted all during the year to extending "peace on earth, good will to all." Our eyes that have been brightened by the star of Christ will, too soon I fear, become dulled to those around us with great need.

Perhaps never in American history has the gap between the rich and poor been any greater. Many people have been left behind in the dizzying pace of the pursuit of profit. On a recent trip to New York City, I went to see that great American icon, the Christmas tree at Rockfeller Center. Alongside the towering, glittering tree, street people and those on the way to the ballet had gathered. Mink stoles brushed against layers of ragged coats huddled around chestnut roasters on the corners of that busy section of Manhattan. Hands clutching shopping bags from exclusive stores hurried past outstretched, hungry hands in the swirl of people there to celebrate or to observe the celebration of others. I felt a great sadness as I realized that the joy of the season depended more on bringing these two groups closer together than on contrasting what each was able to purchase.

Things do not make us happy if we do not have meaningful relationships with others. When we attempt to insulate ourselves from the hurt of others or our own pain, we diminish the chance of building community among people.

Signs of hope emerge, however, such as crocus in late February. Each year in Louisville, Kentucky, a particular foundation provides the Bell Awards, which honor outstanding volunteer work in our county. Senior citizens, single parents, and high school-age students are among the recipients. They volunteer in after school tutoring programs, soup kitchens, services for the blind and hearing impaired, and a multitude of other needed ministries. They offer themselves in these ways because they recognize the significance of building community with those too often forgotten by a success-oriented culture. Not only do they bring hope and joy to those with whom they work, but they realize anew that wholeness in life requires both giving and receiving. As we might imagine, they believe that they get more than they give!

We can only become fully human as persons-in-relation. Like the very being of God, moving outside of ourselves in loving recognition of others makes meaningful the pursuits of humanity.

Endnotes

[1]One of the most thoughtful treatments of the role of vocation (work) is found in James W. Fowler's *Becoming Adult, Becoming Christian* (San Francisco: Harper and Row, 1984) especially chapter four.

[2]Dorothee Sölle, *To Work and To Love* (Philadelphia: Fortress, 1984) 55f., argues that rather than disburdening our work, technology often adds to the image of work as a curse.

[3]Elizabeth Johnson, *Women, Earth and Creator Spirit* (Notre Dame IN: Saint Mary's College, 1993) 53, reminds us that it "is not just individual creatures who are the subject of Spirit-Sophia's life-giving knowledge, but the world as a whole is shaped harmoniously by her guidance."

[4]Warren McWilliams, *Christ and Narcissus* (Scottdale PA: Herald Press, 1992) 75ff., reminds us of the difficulty modern people have acknowledging their utter dependence upon God (and offering thanks) in an age of self-sufficiency.

[5]See Henri J. M. Nouwen, *Lifesigns* (New York: Doubleday, 1986) 55.

[6]In the *City of God* 19.14, 17, Augustine wrote of the Christian as a citizen of the heavenly city, however, "as long as he is in this mortal body, is a pilgrim in a foreign land, away from God."

[7]Although dated, S. Mowinckel's study, *He That Cometh* (Oxford: E. T. Blackwell, 1956) remains a window through which to view the Israelite form of the common oriental royal ideology.

[8]See the article by F. F. Bruce, "Render to Caesar," in *Jesus and the Politics of His Day*, eds. Ernst Bammel and C. F. D. Moule (Cambridge: Cambridge University Press, 1984) 249-63.

[9]See James M. Kittelson, *Luther the Reformer: The Story of the Man and His Career* (Minneapolis: Augsburg, 1986) 145-63, for a fascinating characterization of the relationship between Luther and his protector, Frederick.

[10]Rosemary Radford Ruether, *The Radical Kingdom* (New York: Harper and Row, 1970) 55-74, explores varied Christian utopian attempts at cooperative community.

[11]See Edward Deming Andrews, *The Gift to Be Simple: Songs, Dances, and Rituals of the American Shakers* (New York: J. J. Augustin, 1940).

[12]A helpful introduction is offered by Robert C. Tucker, *Philosophy and Myth in Karl Marx* (Cambridge: Cambridge University Press, 1961).

[13]Dorothee Sölle, *Suffering* (London: Darton, Longman & Todd, 1975); see Wolfhart Pannenberg, *Anthropology in Theological Perspective* (Philadelphia: Westminster, 1985) 275 and J. Michael West, "Eclipse of Meaning: Religion and Self-Discovery in Pannenberg's Recent Thought," *Harvard Divinity Bulletin* 14 (1984): 11-12.

[14]Wendell Berry, *What Are People For?* (San Francisco: North Point Press, 1990) 139-40.

[15]"From the beginning," writes Walter Brueggemann, "the human creature is called, given a vocation, and expected to share in God's work." See his commentary on Genesis in the *Interpretation* series, ed. James Luther Mays (Atlanta: John Knox Press, 1992) 46.

[16]See Sallie McFague's analysis of the ecological crisis of our planet in *The Body of God: An Ecological Theology* (Minneapolis: Fortress Press, 1993).

[17]Sölle, *To Work and To Love*, 63, maintains that this sense of alienation from work often comes from the wage labor system that "pays people to remain silent and to conform to the rules of the game."

[18]Daniel Bell, *The Cultural Contradictions of Capitalism* (New York: Basic Books, 1978) 3-30, warns that the techno-economic order's emphasis on efficiency, profitability, and productivity dominates and controls the defining of virtues and images of personhood.

[19]See Sharon H. Ringe, *Jesus, Liberation, and the Biblical Jubilee* (Philadelphia: Fortress, 1985).

[20]Justice for the poor takes the form of God's compassionate advocacy. See Katie G. Cannon, "The Bible from the Perspective of the Racially and Economically Oppressed," in *Scripture: The Word Beyond the Word* (Women's Division, General Board of Global Ministries, United Methodist Church, 1985) 38.

[21]See Stanley J. Grenz, *Theology for the Community of God* (Nashville: Broadman & Holman, 1994) who maintains that God's central program for creation is the establishment of community.

[22]Grenz, 842, describes the new creation as the "fullness of community."

[23]Wolfhart Pannenberg, "Constructive and Critical Functions of Christian Eschatology," *Harvard Theological Review* 77 (1984): 135-36.

The Suffering and Death of Humanity

Chapter 6

From the very beginning, persons of faith have attempted to reconcile belief in the powerful and loving God with the presence of suffering and death. The fact that human persons suffer and die presents for some a very real obstacle to believing in God. All of us struggle, particularly in the midst of grief, to make sense of this part of human life. Many writers of the twentieth century have suggested that the Christian confession of faith is really quite naive in the face of the human atrocities of our epoch—Auschwitz, Hiroshima, Dachau, Somalia, to mention only a few of the more familiar. Atheistic in orientation, some writers such as Camus, Sartre[1], de Beauvoir, and Russell have rejected the meaningfulness of human life because of these hurtful ambiguities.

Why do people suffer and die? What is the role of pain, both physical and emotional, in our lives? Is death a punishment for our sin or is it a natural outcome for creatures created out of dust? How can we live meaningfully in the face of these inevitable realities? Can they teach us something about the fullness of life, as God intended it? We will explore these and other questions as we reflect on the suffering and death of humanity. We should be warned, however, that rational meaning cannot encompass the mystery of these aspects of human life, as C. S. Lewis' pilgrimage suggests.[2]

A Dusty Existence

To understand the significance of suffering and death, we must note the emphasis the Bible places on the value of life. As a gift from God, we should treasure our lives and the lives of all of God's creatures. To live is to share in the very breath of God, a communion of the most intimate nature (Ps 42:2; 84:2). The breath that proceeds from God also constitutes the breath of our lives, and when we die, it returns to God (Job 34:14). The God of Israel, according to the Hebrew scriptures, is the living God and grants life to both the wicked and the just. Further, Jesus declares that God is "not God of the dead but of the living" (Mark 12:26-27), which suggests a continued experience of the presence of God.

Yet, a person who refuses to live in this relationship with God while alive has already allowed death to encroach upon life. Fullness of life for us as humans means living in conscious gratitude and obedient relationship to our God.[3]

When warning about the consequences of disobedience, God told our human parents in the garden that in the day they would eat of the tree of the knowledge of good and evil, they would "surely die" (Gen 2:17). We know that they did not immediately die but lived to face their disappointed creator, bear children, witness family conflict between two adolescent sons, and endure much of the heartache that we as humans must endure. Thus the word "death" has more than one meaning in the Bible, as our study will show.[4]

The Meaning of Death in Scripture

Many of the scriptural narratives about the deaths of certain persons treat this as a perfectly natural event. Death is not viewed as a punishment, but as the fitting conclusion to a life well lived. Genesis recounts Abraham's death in this manner:

> This is the length of Abraham's life, one hundred seventy-five years. Abraham breathed his last and died in a good old age, an old man and full of years, and was gathered to his people. (25:7-8)

The description of the death of Isaac, his son, is similar, "And Isaac breathed his last; he died and was gathered to his people, old and full of days; and his sons Esau and Jacob buried him" (35:29). These deaths were not an interruption to life, but the expected outcome of aging—being "full of years."[5]

While the biblical writers acknowledged the inevitability of death of all persons, we must remember that they distinguished whether one died a "good" death or a "bad" death. The kind of death had much influence as to how death was received and was linked to the kind of life one lived. A person had responsibility, to a major extent, for the kind of death he or she died. The different value ascribed to the different kinds of death are illuminating, for these insights can help guide us in our living and preparation for death.

Life in its fullness possessed health, prosperity, children, favor of God, honor and respect in society, and length of days. All of these factors contributed to a "good" death, which was reserved for the righteous. One of Job's "friends," Eliphaz, articulated the content of this death, "You shall come to your grave in ripe old age, as a shock of grain comes up to the threshing floor in its season" (Job 5:26).[6] The attainment of wisdom, an opportunity to mature, seeing one's family multiply, and life-long enjoyment of the presence of the Lord were aspects of this kind of death. A death could also be identified as good due to the proper burial and mourning. Thus, a person's children had a part in making the experience of death "good." Those of us who have buried an elderly parent or grandparent know of the importance of strong family support during their waning years.

Usually the "bad" death meant premature death that was the result of foolish or rebellious living or a death that meant the person could not complete certain goals in life. The wisdom writers considered the "bad" death to be the logical outcome of the wicked.[7] As one of the biblical aphorisms put it, "Getting gain by violence takes away the life of its possessors" (Prov 1:19). "A person's folly could hasten death" was the recurring warning throughout the Proverbs. The Book of Job describes how "[the godless] die in their youth, and their life ends in shame" (36:14). A "bad" death could also refer to a violent death that could mean a lessened chance for proper burial. Further, when one died without an heir, the sting of death was great because one's memory was forgotten and there was no extension of his or her life into the future.[8]

Hence, a person must choose the way of life that will allow a quality and a longevity that can make possible a "good" death. "Whoever is steadfast in righteousness will live, but whoever pursues evil will die" (Prov 11:19). These warnings and admonitions contain a timeless wisdom that we should also heed.

Another perspective on death develops in the Old Testament that regards it as "absurd" or a "vanity," the word found in the Book of Ecclesiastes (1:2). Death is beyond human power to control; "No one has power . . . over the day of death" (Eccl 8:8). Further, the writer grimly depicted the dead as knowing "nothing; they have no more reward, and even the memory of them is lost" (9:4-5).

As awareness of the significance of the individual's relationship to God came to focus, however, the biblical writers began to insist that it is unfitting that death should interrupt God's loving relationship to the creature.[9] Indeed, the mortality of the human being became a burning theological problem in the Old Testament only when righteous persons face the threat of untimely death. Job lamented that death meant that God could no longer be involved with him. "Now I shall lie in the earth; you will seek me, but I shall not be" (Job 7:21).

If death is the limit to human life and all of our loving relationships, then despair is the proper response, according to this biblical philosopher. He sounds a bit like the time-worn song sung by Peggy Lee, "If That's All There Is." Why not eat, drink, and be merry?—if that's all there is. The main accent of the Hebrew scriptures, however, does not allow the reality of death to call the meaning of life into question, as in so much modern Western thought.[10]

The Scriptures also view death as retribution or punishment for sin. One strand of the Old Testament sees death as punishment for the shedding of another's blood (Gen. 9:5-6). As the biblical narrative continues, however, not only murderers are so condemned, but all persons stand under the penalty of death because of their disobedience to God; and without the sin of our forebears, humans would not have to die. "Death," in this instance, means more than simply the cessation of life. It is a metaphor for life in rebellion against God, a walking death. Turning away from the living God is a death sentence. Because of our sin, death as the natural end of one's life becomes a powerful shadow that can darken all of one's days. Reflecting a deep awareness of this lurking potential, the apostle Paul wrote, "The wages of sin is death" (Rom 6:23).[11]

The death of Jesus Christ transforms the meaning of death for persons of faith.[12] Until Jesus' life, death, and resurrection, we could not have an assurance of life after death. Although the hope of resurrection can be seen in the Old Testament and also in the intertestamental writings, Jesus' experience and its interpretation by the New Testament writers offers a concrete basis for our hope.

The Meaning of Suffering in Scripture

The biblical writers for the most part viewed human suffering with the same sort of equanimity with which they viewed death. Although one may choose to live wisely and, thereby, avoid some of the consequences of folly, there is a degree of unpredictability about human suffering. It is a part of being human.

Our ancestors did not live with the notion that pain or suffering is to be avoided at all costs, like we attempt to do. Western

culture constantly seeks a pain-free way of life, which is certainly
an elusive and inappropriate dream. One of the results of this illu-
sion is a society sorely tempted by drugs that will enable us to "feel
good" constantly.[13] We cannot totally avoid pain and suffering,
however, and we should not believe that it is possible.

First, we must remember that even though God does not send
human suffering, we can question God about it. Many people live
with either a punitive view of God or a kind of fatalism about suffering and death. You and I have heard people say, "God won't put
more upon us than we can bear." Although this belief affirms
God's care for us, it assumes that God receives some sort of divine
satisfaction out of inflicting misery on wayward humans. The
Bible continually speaks of the God that loves us, walks with us,
and desires that no one be crushed by suffering and pain. One can
agree with Rabbi Kushner's insistence that "things" do not happen
to people because they are bad; we should attend to his reticence
to merely draw a simple correlation between human suffering and
particular acts.[14]

We might ask, "Doesn't the Book of Job teach that God sends
suffering to 'test' the righteous?" As we know, this enigmatic book
has been the subject of numerous commentaries, essays, and stage
plays each seeking to understand its insights on the relationship of
innocent human suffering to the will of God.

This poet-theologian boldly challenged an earlier theological
strand in Israel, that of the Book of Deuteronomy, which maintained that the good person is rewarded with material prosperity
and the wicked is punished with temporal suffering. The story of
Job turned that idea on its head. The suffering Job maintained his
integrity as one who had not turned his back on God, even
though his friends were suspicious and suggested that he should
not question or challenge God. Mrs. Job, who had skipped the
courses in psychology and pastoral care, urged him to "curse God
and die"—hardly words of comfort. Nevertheless, Job was exon-
erated and stood before God as an intercessor for his friends. None

of the characters in the story, including Job, really had an adequate view of God, as the book clearly teaches.

Perhaps we read with understanding when we perceive that the suffering righteous stand in the presence of God who addresses and cares for them in the midst of it.[15] Indeed, the "cry of absence"[16] does not ultimately go unheard.

Second, suffering arises from the conditions of an unfinished world and human sin.[17] I have put these two aspects of suffering in this order intentionally, for some persons, such as Job's friends, will always find a way to blame the victim. In Jesus' day, the question about the blind man was "Who sinned, this man or his parents?" (John 9:1-2). Jesus refused to see sin as the source of all sickness and suffering.

When God began creating, God's purpose was not to call a ready-made world into being. When God declared that the world was good, that did not mean it was finished, but that it was suitable for God's purpose, which included a well prepared place for human beings. It also meant that the process of life involves pain. Perhaps a stanza of Tennyson's poem *In Memoriam* expresses this context that involves both hope and suffering,

> Are God and nature then at strife,
> That Nature lends such evil dream?
> So careful of the type she seems,
> So careless of the single life.

Pain or suffering can actually be more of a friend to be embraced than an enemy to be shunned if we probe its origin and usefulness. They are part of the rhythms of life established by God, and though they are, at times, exceedingly hard to bear, we should not run from them. Whether physical or emotional, suffering grows out of the structures of created, limited, interdependent reality. Because we are not naturally immortal, pain can warn us of threats to our bodies, stresses and illnesses that demand attention.

Some of these adverse circumstances we bring upon ourselves; others are the cost of a relatively independent world where randomness in the natural processes make possible our freedom. As Kushner writes: "God leaves us room to be human."[18] If everything were determined ahead of time, how could we freely choose to become what God wants us to be? Yet, sometimes this indeterminacy results in human deformity and unexpected suffering.[19]

I remember walking through the neonatal critical care unit at a large hospital in Dallas where a friend of mine was serving as chaplain. As I looked at the tiny bits of humanity lying under protective sheets of plastic, I wondered at the cause of their precarious existence. Some of the babies were born to addicted mothers, so we might say that wrong choices—sin—played a role in their suffering; but others simply represented the random unpredictability of the gene pool or a troubled pregnancy. Such is the result of the delicate web of life[20] in which children with Down's syndrome or spina bifida can be born.

The Book of Romans speaks about the "groaning of creation," the suffering existence of all living things waiting for liberation. The text (8:20) contends that God purposed for the world to live in such ambiguity, yet not without hope. Because God's spirit is in the world, we can live with a faith in what we do not yet see.

Yes, some suffering does arise out of human sinning—promiscuous living, abuse of the body, and fits of destructive rage, to mention only a few. Are the hurts that follow sent by God? I believe that the biblical teaching about the "wrath of God" has more do to with reaping the consequences of our actions than with God manufacturing the AIDS virus or emphysema or liver disease to punish us. These maladies can arise from destructive behaviors, however, so we should renounce the idea of sickness as punishment for sin.[21]

Third, suffering can build character, but it can also paralyze the human spirit. I often hear the would-be pious speaking about the patience "God can teach one through suffering," or how God is using this tactic in the making of a saint. Unfortunately, this seems to make the ends justify the means.[22] Of course, we can learn about our finitude and mortality through suffering and feel more deeply our dependence upon God and others. Suffering also can be a crushing experience, however, and we should not overly spiritualize another's suffering.

We are neither to seek suffering or flee it. An early church father, Polycarp, was enamored with martyrdom. He thought that he would be a saint if he suffered to the point of death for his faith. Well, he got his wish after inviting persecution for many years, but being burned at the stake at age eighty-six was not his notion of going down in a blaze of glory!

To seek suffering is to be a masochist, and there is that strain in Christianity. To deny suffering a legitimate part in reality is to be apathetic, incapable of suffering or feeling—a passionless existence.[23] Medicine offers many ways to control suffering, yet it should be suspicious of the myth of suffering-free human living.

Suffering and the Goodness of God

Pain and suffering are no strangers to God. The message of the Bible clearly speaks of the pain God feels when a covenant partner rejects the loving relationship God extends to us. Scripture reverberates with a dirge-like cadence the sense of loss God feels when forsaken for idols (Isa 54:6ff).

Pain and suffering accompany the loss of relationship or squandered opportunity. To be able to feel this is another dimension of being created in the image of God. If we could not feel pain or suffer, we could not love, for love always involves the possibility of hurt or rejection. If we could not mourn personal loss, we would not value our relationships and we would be less than personal.[24] Our ability to feel pain also reminds us of the deep hurt we inflict upon others and upon God.

According to the Bible, God suffers with us and ultimately redeems suffering. Not only does God provide companionship in human suffering through the ever-present spirit of God, but also through those of us called to heal a hurting world. We are God's tangible presence with those who suffer, for God's presence is always a mediated presence. In humility, God allows us to represent the holy presence with others through our skill, caring, and sustaining human presence.

The foundation of our faith as Christians is that through Jesus, that human being who lived fully for others and for God, God has proclaimed once and for all that human suffering is not meaningless and that one can die in hope. Jesus assures us that our existence matters greatly to God, for surely we are more than sparrows and flowers of the field. We are called to a fundamental trust in God's care, especially during suffering, for God is never absent from our pain. God suffers with all of creation and most acutely in the death of the Son on the cross.[25]

Our suffering is best borne in community. The Stone Center for Developmental Services in Massachusetts has pioneered in the study of the significance of community for health. According to this organization's research, our health derives from mutually empathic and empowering relationships. These astute clinicians and theorists are attempting to shift the primary therapeutic emphasis away from focus on the individual and more toward growth-producing relationships. Thus, we must be present to the suffering of others if we wish to assist in another's healing, which is only possible if we have learned to acknowledge and bear our own suffering.

We are called to suffer with others. This can be an integral part of the healing and sustaining process and is an important aspect of being fully human. The word "compassion" literally means to suffer with—a patient mercy. Most of us are impatient, with others and with ourselves. Suffering with another requires slow, careful attentiveness. Healing has its own schedule, and we must respect the processes God has inscribed in our world. As we know, persons do not always get well, but our presence can give joy and companionship as our loved ones move toward the valley of the shadow of death.

When I was a graduate student, a friend of mine died of cancer. She was a bright, delightful "thirty-something" woman who planned to be a professor of Old Testament. Her husband was a faithful presence at her side, struggling to be strong in the midst of bleak prospects. Several of her friends decided that we would take turns sitting with her in the hospital. During those long hours as she drifted between sleep and waking, she offered us some of her best gifts. She encouraged each of us in our goals, and she would not let us feel sorry for her. Instead of saying "Why is this happening to me?" she murmured, "Why not me? I can bear this." Although she was deeply grieved that her life was being cut short, she continued to nurture the relationships surrounding her. Together we journeyed toward her death, but not without hope.

The Significance of Death Awareness

Death holds a great significance in our culture. It presses in upon all of us even though we try to escape its inevitability. Many of us delay making wills because we really do not want to think about the fact that we will someday die. However far we progress as human beings in securing our biological nature, we can never really escape certain constraints of the physical basis of our lives. Created out of dust, we cannot expect to live forever.

The size of a human being, for instance, is limited by the physical structure of the body. The body is such that under favorable conditions it might function for about eighty years, more or less, but there comes a time when it wears out. Better medical care keeps most of us going longer today than once would have been the case, but the extent to which human life can be extended is actually quite limited.

No doubt you have read of persons who have incurable diseases who are contemplating being "frozen" until the time when a cure might be found. This is a form of "death-denial" that is unwilling to live with human limitations. Who would want to awake to learn that all of one's friends and relatives have died at an approximately normal age, and only you are left? Besides, I have always worried that someone might unplug the refrigerator by accident!

Outwardly, the death of an animal and the death of a human being might seem the same. In each case, disease or injury or old age has so disabled the organism that life comes to an end. There is an important difference, however. We know that we will die, and we live in the face of death. Dobhansky calls this knowledge "death awareness" and claims that it is one of the basic characteristics of humans as a biological species.

Other creatures live more from moment to moment, but the human being who is aware of death becomes also aware of life as a whole, as a dynamic movement of life from birth to death. This helps us to think of time in a different way, as a limited epoch in which we can create a meaningful life.[26] Because death enters our field of awareness, our lives are more distinctively human. We realize that our choices matter and that we do not have forever to make up our minds about key issues in our lives.

The great philosopher Heidegger was so impressed by the difference between the end of an animal's life and the end of human life that he proposed the use of different words. The end of the life of an animal is "perishing," he suggested, while "death," strictly speaking, only comes to the human being.[27] Death is a personal event for us, whether it be the death of a loved one or our own anticipated death. More than anything else, death gives us a sense of the finitude and even the precariousness of human existence.

Different historical periods have addressed this aspect of our lives as humans in markedly different ways. Some generations in earlier times have lived with a brooding awareness of death's proximity, especially during the years of plagues when the majority of the population might die or when the death rate of children outstripped the birth rate. The symbols of death were ever present in the art and architecture of the churches; gargoyles and the devil depicted the powerful presence of death. Other more secure generations have cultivated a death-denying environment in which death is hardly to be mentioned, and when we do speak of it, we use euphemisms such as "passed away" or "no longer with us" to lessen the stark reality.

During periods of war, our awareness of death is greatly heightened. In the past few years we have seen countless young men and women sent to the Persian Gulf, Somalia, and Haiti. Families ripped apart by the threat of war are facing the possibility that their loved ones may not return home. Death has entered their horizons in a forceful way.

Even when we refuse to contemplate our own death, there is a vicarious experience of death when others die. Who put it more poignantly than John Donne?

> Here the bells can scarce solemnize the funeral of any person, but that I knew him, or knew that he was my neighbor. We dwelt in houses near to one another before, but now he is going into that house into which I must follow him.... No man is an island, entire of itself; every man is a piece of the continent, a part of the mainland. If a clod be washed away by the sea, Europe is the less.... Any man's death diminishes me, because I am involved in mankind; and therefore never send to know for whom the bell tolls; it tolls for thee.[28]

Donne viewed our involvement in the whole of humankind in a manner akin to the biblical revelation. Our lives are bound up together. Thus, our identity as a part of all humanity means that the death of another reminds us of our own impending death.

Death as Friend and Enemy

We should view death in its positive as well as its negative character, for death can be both friend and enemy. Death that comes through giving one's life for another is particularly significant. Jesus said, "No one has greater love than this, to lay down one's life for one's friends" (John 15:13). Jesus was the exemplary "friend" through his poured-out life for others. Each of us can think of selfless actions in which a person has risked or faced death to protect the life and human dignity of others.

I have always been moved by Victor Hugo's novel, *The Hunchback of Notre Dame*. Quasimodo, a person shunned because of his deformity, spent his life among the bells of the old cathedral, ringing them with such vigor that he had gradually grown deaf. Once when he was flogged in public, a young woman named Esmerelda took pity on him and offered him a drink of water. Quasimodo never forgot her kindness and repaid her by offering his life to save her. As Jesus taught us, some things (persons) are worth dying for.

At times death can be a welcome friend when a person's suffering has grown too intense to bear any longer. As we sat beside the bed of my friend dying of cancer, we encouraged her to let herself be welcomed into the arms of God. "You don't have to keep struggling," we told her. "It's all right just to let yourself drift on out into eternity." Though it was painful to say goodbye, it was more painful for us to watch her suffer. Death came as release and sanctuary for her.

Yet, we can never ignore the threatening power of death as enemy. The apostle Paul spoke of sin and death reigning over us since the time of Adam (Rom 5:12-21). Sin enslaves one in a "body of death" (Rom 7:5-25). Death is the "last enemy" (1 Cor 15:26, 54-56). Even Jesus faced death with a sense of horror and revulsion, as his struggle in Gethsemane and his cry of dereliction on the cross (Mark 15:34) revealed. But Jesus waged battle against the power of death. Hebrews reflects at length on this theme.

> Since therefore the children share flesh and blood, he himself likewise shared the same things, so that through death he might destroy the one who has the power of death, that is, the devil, and free those who all their lives were held in slavery by the fear of death....In the days of his flesh, Jesus offered up prayers and supplications, with loud cries and tears, to the one who was able to save him from death. (Heb 2:14-15; 5:7)

The story does not end here, however. Jesus conquered death, which makes it possible for us to face death without regarding it as a fearsome enemy.[29] Jesus lived again after dying! That must surely mean that all the human yearnings for life after death can now be realized. Death does not have to mean separation from the source of life. Persons do not have to lead some weak, dusty existence under the domination of some alien power, as the Old Testament writers believed (Prov 21:16; Job 26:5; Eccl 3:20).

In lyrical form in 1 Corinthians 15:54-57, Paul celebrated this astonishing new event in human history:

> Death has been swallowed up in victory! Where, O death, is thy victory? Where, O death, is thy sting? Thanks be to God, who gives us the victory through our Lord Jesus Christ.

The early Christians believed that they could withstand whatever might come, for through Christ's resurrection they were assured that neither death, nor life, nor angels, nor rulers, nor things present, nor things to come, nor powers, nor height, nor depth, nor anything else in all creation, will be able to separate us from the love of God in Christ Jesus our Lord. (Rom 8:38-39)

As history records, those Christians faced lions, tyrants such as Nero, extreme poverty, and other severe hardships with faithful confidence because of their trust in the God who had raised Christ Jesus from the dead. Suffering and death were to be expected, for the "servant is not greater than the master."

Like those early believers, our lives find their meaning through the life and death of Jesus. We can face our own painful interludes because of our faith in the God of our Lord Jesus Christ through whom we are "more than conquerors" (Rom 8:37).

Perhaps I have learned this lesson best through the witness of some of the older members of our congregation. At our Christmas Eve communion service recently, my family sat behind three widows. It was an icy evening—none of them really needed to be facing hazardous driving and the potential of breaking a hip through a nasty spill—but there they were singing, greeting others, and preventing their friends from experiencing isolated loneliness. I marvelled at their spunk and obvious faith. Each of them had experienced a tough year. One had lost her husband to heart failure; another was grieving the death of a granddaughter, killed by a drunk driver; the other shed silent tears over a grandson stricken with AIDS. These women, the very spine of our church, came to offer prayer and thanksgiving to God for the Christ child and friendship to all of us who look to them as models of faithfulness.

Suffering and death will come to all of us, but as persons of faith, we can face them in confidence because God will walk with us through them. One of my favorite hymns is "God Will Take Care of You," written by Civilla D. Martin. I love it because it tells the truth about those of us who put unwavering trust in God. We can "be not dismayed whate'er betide" because of the one "who never leaves us or forsakes us." Thanks be to God!

Endnotes

[1]Specifically, Jean-Paul Sartre, *Being and Nothingness* (New York: Philosophical Library, 1956).

[2]In his optimistic *The Problem of Pain* (London: Geoffrey Bles, The Centenary Press, 1940) C. S. Lewis believed every occurrence within human experience can be reasonably comprehended, suffering included. Approximately twenty-one years later, after the death of his beloved wife (who had suffered the excruciating pain of bone cancer), *A Grief Observed* (New York: Bantam Books, 1961) made no such claim.

[3]"Life" as relatedness and "death" as relationless is stressed by Eberhard Jüngel, *Death: The Riddle and the Mystery* (Philadelphia: Westminster, 1974).

[4]See especially Lloyd R. Bailey, Sr., *Biblical Perspectives on Death* (Philadelphia: Fortress, 1979).

[5]As Walther Zimmerli, *The Old Testament and the World* (Atlanta: John Knox Press, 1976) 177, writes: "The threat is never the simple possibility of death through old."

[6]See Dorothee Sölle, *Suffering* (London: Darton, Longman & Todd, 1975) 109-19, for contrasting interpretations of the suffering of Job.

[7]The "cursed" death of Jesus on the cross proved a stumbling block to those steeped in this understanding of retributive justice.

[8]See Claus Westermann, *Blessing: In the Bible and the Life of the Church* (Philadelphia: Fortress, 1978).

[9]A good introduction to the transition toward apocalyptic eschatology is found in George Nickelsburg, *Resurrection, Immorality, and Eternal Life in Intertestamental Judaism*, Harvard Theological Studies (Cambridge: Harvard university Press, 1972) 26.

[10]Bailey, 52.

[11]Paul greatly expanded the understanding of death: It is everything within creation that deviates from the Creator's design. Hence the movement of the world is "death-ward."

[12]Douglas John Hall, *God and Human Suffering* (Minneapolis: Augsburg, 1986) 93, refers to this transformation as "conquest from within."

[13]Leszek Kolakowski, *Presentness of Myth*, describes our world as a "culture of analgesics" and speaks of a "headlong flight from suffering," a "narcotizing of life." Cited by D. Sölle in *The Strength of the Weak* (Philadelphia: Westminster, 1984) 24.

[14]Rabbi Kushner, *When Bad Things Happen to Good People* (New York: Avon, 1983) 53.

[15]See Paul Fiddes, *The Creative Suffering of God* (Oxford: Clarendon Press, 1988).

[16]See Martin Marty, *A Cry of Absence* (San Francisco: Harper & Row, 1983).

[17]Hall speaks of suffering as "becoming" within a processive creation and suffering as "burden" because of human sinfulness.

[18]Kushner, 72ff.

[19]See Edward Farley, *Good and Evil: Interpreting a Human Condition* (Minneapolis: Fortress, 1990) 76ff.

[20]Arthur Peacocke, *Creation and the World of Science* (Oxford: Clarendon Press, 1979) 160ff.

[21]Daniel Liderbach, *Why Do We Suffer?* (New York: Paulist Press, 1992) 125, denounces the theological tendency to interpret the experience of suffering to be the consequence of sin. He writes: "There is no analytical cause that humans can identify as the source of suffering. No cause, not even sin . . . can be identified as the explanation for suffering in the life of anyone."

[22]Many have criticized John Hick's perspective in *Evil and the God of Love*, rev. ed. (San Francisco: Harper & Row, 1978) for his "instrumental" view of evil; specifically, it contributes to the "making of souls."

[23]Indeed, the cross suggests that "suffering can be conceived of ontologically as an expression . . . of care for others," Johnson, *She Who Is*, (New York: Crossroad, 1992) 265.

[24]I have been pointed by my research student, Mark Medley, to the significant work of contemporary orthodox theologian John D. Zizioulas. His *Being as Communion* argues that authentic personhood is only constituted by relationship. (Crestwood NY: St. Vladimir's Seminary Press, 1993)

[25]William C. Placher, *Narratives of a Vulnerable God* (Louisville KY: Westminster/John Knox, 1994) 18, maintains that God can help only because God "acts out of love, and love risks suffering."

[26]See the insightful work of Daniel Yankelovich, *New Rules: Searching for Self-Fulfillment in a World Turned Upside Down* (New York: Random House, 1981) chaps. 3-5.

[27]See Heidegger's magisterial *Being and Time*, trans. J. Macquarrie and E. Robinson (Oxford: Basil Blackwell, 1962).

[28]See *The Complete Poetry and Selected Prose of John Donne*, ed. Charles M. Coffin (New York: The Modern Library, 1952).

[29]Alister E. McGrath, *Christian Theology* (Oxford: Blackwell Publishers, 1994) 335f., suggests that the resurrection of Jesus Christ assumes a number of functions within Christian theology at the eschatological level; it undergirds the Christian hope of eternal life.

The Hope of Humanity

Chapter 7

Human beings must live in hope, or we cannot continue. Perhaps no one has expressed this fact more starkly than John Macquarrie: "If hope were totally extinguished and there remained only despair, it would be impossible to go on living."[1] All of us are oriented to the future. Even the casual question, "What's for dinner?" is a reminder that hope abides—unless it is meatloaf! Each of us lives in a process of change, and hope motivates us to strive toward achieving our yearnings and goals.

Many young persons, however, have a difficult time engaging the future. Our culture demands instant gratification and, thus, makes it harder to wait for certain privileges and experiences. Further, ever since the devastation wrought in the second world war, we consciously live in the shadow of the "bomb." When the United States bombed Libya, this was brought keenly to mind for me, especially the effect upon teenagers.

One of my teaching colleagues at the seminary, the father of an eighth grade daughter, was out of town at the time the bombing occurred. He was totally unprepared for the trauma that this event caused his daughter. Frantic with fear, she finally managed to reach him where he was staying. She was impressed that somehow this military strike would precipitate World War III, the dreaded nuclear holocaust. As she tearfully described her feelings, he realized that she lived with a sense of despair about the future, not at all sure that she would live to be an adult. Fear was threatening to eclipse hope for her.

A genuine and realistic hope is usually rather fragile because of our awareness of the ambiguities of the future. Those of us who maintain hope in the face of the future will probably also have known, at times, the alternative mood of fear. One of the most striking features of our lives as humans is that on the whole, even when the threats are nearly overwhelming, hope seems to pre-dominate over fear.[2]

One of the most popular songs from the musical play *Porgy and Bess* is "Ole Man River." The bass soloist thunders out the words, "I'm tired of living and scared of dying." His words express the feelings of many people, especially those for whom hope is dim. Henry David Thoreau wrote that every person at some point feels a "sense of quiet desperation," which leads us to whether this has to be the dominant feeling, or can we keep hope alive in our troubled world?

Perhaps the beginning point is to ask "What is hope?" What are its sources, and for what do we as humans hope? For peace? For all our wants and needs to be met? Do we hope that our lives will take on a greater significance than this short life on earth will allow? Do all persons have hope, or is this a unique perspective of the Christian? In this chapter, we explore these dimensions of hope.

Biblical Perspectives on Hope

Hope in the Bible is the expectation and longing for the future that only God can provide. The prophet Jeremiah gathered up much of the Old Testament tradition when he proclaimed,

> O hope of Israel! O Lord! All who forsake you shall be put to shame; those who turn away from you shall be recorded in the underworld, for they have forsaken the fountain of living water, the Lord. (17:13)

One of my favorite assurances about the future is Jeremiah's declaration, "For I surely know the plans I have for you, says the Lord, plans for your welfare and not for harm, to give you a future with hope" (29:11).

The psalmist also expressed the anchor of one's hope in God. "For you, O Lord, are my hope, my trust, O Lord, from my youth" (71:5). Because of God's faithful loving-kindness, the people of Israel believed that God could be trusted to ensure their future. Again, the psalmist testified to the confidence one can have in God, "Truly, the eye of the Lord is on those who fear him, on those who hope in his steadfast love" (33:18). The words used to describe God—rock, refuge, protector—speak of stability and security.

As we know, Israel was often tempted to put her trust in other than God. At times, the nation trusted more in its military strength, "horses and chariots," than in the faithfulness of God who called this people to be a "holy nation," unlike their warmongering neighbors. Speaking for God, prophets would recall the nation to its true destiny, specifically to trust in the one who alone could secure the promised future of peace. At times, this was very hard to believe, for the enemies of Israel were many, and the period of exile was harsh.

The prophets reminded Israel that God would perform an act of deliverance so great in magnitude that it was comparable to creation itself.[3] Through the prophet Isaiah, the Lord said, "For I am about to create new heavens and a new earth; the former things shall not be remembered" (65:17). The prophet of the exile was the clear voice that reminded the people that God had not forsaken them.

> Do not remember the former things, or consider the things of old. I am about to do a new thing; now it springs forth, do you not perceive it? I will make a way in the wilderness and rivers in the desert. (43:18-19)

God promised the people of Israel return from exile and a pros-
perous life once again in their homeland. What seemed an
impossible dream to them was within God's power.

The prophetic tradition envisioned a transformed future in
which creation would be brought to completion and all of God's
creatures would live in harmony.

> The wolf and the lamb shall feed together, the lion shall eat
> straw like the ox; but the serpent—its food shall be dust! They
> shall not hurt or destroy on all my holy mountain, says the
> Lord. (Isa 65:25)

Members of the holy nation wondered when this state of
peace would occur. Would it actually happen in their lifetime, or
was it a long way in the future? The promise of "a new heaven and
a new earth" sounded as though God might have to start over with
creation. Would the present world be destroyed? Questions such
as these occupied the writers in the late period of the writing of
the Old Testament and especially during the intertestamental
period.

Indeed, these questions were still a part of the religious conversation during the time of Jesus.[4] Some of them are our
questions also. We wonder if our present world will be destroyed
by a nuclear bomb or our ecological negligence. Who has the
power to destroy the world? During biblical times, people believed
that only God had such power. We now know that "the end of the
world" is, sadly, within human reach through our devastating
technology that can bring total annihilation to the earth and all of
its creatures.[5] Yet, God promises a future and a hope.

The preaching of Jesus was filled with a message of hopeful
anticipation, which was a continuation of the Old Testament
prophecies about the time when God's peace would prevail.
Mark's Gospel begins its account of the ministry of Jesus with
these words,

> Jesus came to Galilee, proclaiming the good news of God, and saying, "The time is fulfilled, and the kingdom of God has come near; repent, and believe in the good news." (14-15)

Moreover, all of Jesus' preaching is filled with the same accent on the "rule of God" that is drawing near and has, in fact, begun in Jesus' compassionate acts toward the sick and outcast.

The "kingdom" of which Jesus so frequently spoke was a kind of joyful existence in which everything was reversed. The captives would go free, the mighty would be cast down, persons would be welcomed that the "religious" despised. The "good news" Jesus brought was his affirmation that God is willing to receive all those who are willing to repent and believe. A person's race, gender, or economic level could neither qualify nor disqualify for membership in this new society based upon relationship to Jesus. They were now included in a community of suffering and hope.[6]

Not only did Jesus promise that a new kind of life was possible for those who followed him without reservation, but he promised that their lives were securely in his safe-keeping. His words in the Gospel of John were difficult for early Christians to understand, and yet they provided for those persons, and for us, an abiding comfort as death approaches.

> Do not let your hearts be troubled. Believe in God, believe also in me. In my Father's house there are many dwelling places. If it were not so, would I have told you that I go to prepare a place for you? And if I go and prepare a place for you, I will come again and will take you to myself, so that where I am, there you may be also. (14:1-3)

Jesus assured believers that their security is in being with him and that he will make that possible, both in life and in death.

The most developed concept of hope, however, is found in the Pauline letters. Paul frequently used the word hope, along with faith and love, as emblematic of the new life in Christ. The faithful person can be "confident" (2 Cor 5:6) because the hope that is constantly nourished by the presence of the Spirit of the risen Lord in the life of the Christian will not be disappointed. Hope assures the believers that the journey that they began in their baptism will be consummated in their own resurrection, after the likeness of Christ (Rom 11:22; 1 Cor 15:2).

Paul described the resurrection of Jesus as "the first fruits of those who have died" (1 Cor 15:20). "First fruits," an agricultural metaphor, means the guarantee that other fruits will follow. As an accomplished Old Testament scholar, Paul knew that the "first"— whether it be child, crops, or animal—had a special status because it was sanctified for God and suggested God's ownership and sovereignty over all the earth. The first serves as an example or paradigm on what can be expected. Paul used this common saying as a way of expressing that just as God raised Jesus from the dead, we, too, can count on being raised with him just as we have already "been risen to walk in newness of life" through our baptism (Rom 6:4).

The Christian hope is that our salvation will reach its goal when our lives are transformed through resurrection from the dead.[7] What we have begun in this life (Rom 5:1-3), the "hope of sharing the glory of God" cannot be completed until the final "redemption of our bodies" (Rom 8:23), which is Paul's way of saying that our embodied existence as human beings will continue through the grace and power of God. Along with the salvation of human beings, "the creation itself will be set free from its bondage to decay and will obtain the freedom of the glory of the children of God" (Rom 8:19-21).

Throughout Paul's writings and those of other early Christians, Jesus serves as the anchor for Christian hope. The author of Hebrews wrote,

> We have this hope, a sure and steadfast anchor of the soul, a hope that enters the inner shrine behind the curtain, where Jesus, a forerunner on our behalf, has entered. (6:19-20)

Thus, we need not fear to walk the pathway of persecution or death because Jesus has already gone before us and makes our passage safe. Our hope for wholeness in this life and for an enduring significance to our lives is anchored in Jesus Christ.

The Function of Hope

Hope plays an important role in everyday life. At this level, most of our hopes do not even find expression in words, but they are certainly implied in the future-oriented actions that we take. When we plant a tree or build a house, take a course in college, marry a spouse, or bring children into the world, we are acting in hope. Such acts demonstrate a basic trust in the future, although our hopes are sometimes frustrated.

Yet our actions show that we believe it is worthwhile to continue trusting in the future, and that our freedom and creativeness allow us a share in the shaping and transforming of our world. Hope requires a patient yearning and working toward the possible good of the future and requires imagination that allows us to think about never-before-realized opportunities.[8]

In many respects, hope has the character of a gift. We cannot summon it through sheer determination or will, for God has crafted it into the fiber of our beings as humans and as something given firm definition through Christ. Thus, we cannot remain hopeful if we are enslaved by working toward our goals. We need to cultivate other aspects of our lives as well.

"All work and no play makes Jack a dull boy," the old saying goes, and we might add, "It doesn't do any more for Jane, either." Our play, humor, and laughter contribute greatly to our hope. Most of us take ourselves far too seriously. We either think that we have to work all the time to be worth anything, or we despair that our work will ever get us anywhere. Often we allow the seriousness of our work to diminish our sense of humor and capacity for play and laughter. We need to reconsider the value these graces can have in our lives.[9]

Those of us who are hard-driving in our work often bring this same determination to our play. Thus, it is not surprising that many heart attacks and accidents occur on the weekend when we are going to have a good time if it kills us! Our frantic "leisure" activities show how driven we really are. It shows especially when we take up a new sport or hobby, for few of us are content simply to be an amateur. "Amateur" sounds to us like a clumsy person who does not know the right end of a golf club or how to keep score in tennis, but actually the word "amateur" was originally a French word that meant someone who pursues an activity for the love of it.

I recently attended the funeral of a ninety-three-year-old woman, a remarkable member of our church and community. During the eulogy, her colorful life was mentioned. She took up golf at age seventy-five. The pro at her golf course kept quizzing her about her age and why she would even consider learning a new sport when others were more content to protect their brittle bones. She simply said, "Well, I may not make the pro circuit, but I will learn something about golf for the love of it." He, like many of us, struggled to understand such a motive.

To be an amateur is a way to enjoy a new activity without feeling that we have to be the "best" or that such is a waste of time. For a short time we can put aside or at least readjust our competitive attitudes and simply allow ourselves the pleasure of recreating play. Our physical well-being is a matter of stewardship and a worthy pursuit. Exercise, diversion, and relaxation can all contribute to a perspective in which hope remains a constant.[10]

Though I hate to admit it, by nature I am a competitive person. I have continued to play the sport I played competitively in high school: tennis. Three other women and I regularly play doubles a couple of times a week. Too stingy to join a tennis club that provides indoor courts, we play about ten months out of the year on public courts. We are fairly evenly matched (although craft of mind does have to engage the younger knees of my opponents), and we all regularly win and lose because we switch teams nearly every set. This helps us remember that we play because we enjoy the sport and being together more than we enjoy always defeating the other team.

Humor, like grace, reminds us that we are imperfect persons to whom calamities and misadventures will inevitably occur. When we allow our laughter—especially our ability to laugh at ourselves—to accompany our bumbling incidents, it can be a healing balm for our need to be in control of all circumstances. It can also be a graceful and non-intimidating way of instructing others that human failing does not have to erase hope. Authentic hope, as many contemporary psychologists believe, does not exist in a vacuum, but rather in shared experiences with others. Humor and laughter are ways of establishing common bonds and a deeper intimacy with persons who, like us, need encouragement through mutuality. As my colleague Andy Lester often reminds me, life-giving love offered to others promotes hope.

Recently a hospital in our city held a seminar on the role of humor and laughter in health. Medical studies demonstrate how laughter can relieve stress and allow one's body to function better. I was grateful to see this important aspect of our lives as humans given its proper therapeutic value. We read in Proverbs 15:13, "A merry heart does one good, like a medicine." Which would you rather take: a hearty laugh or a spoonful of a foul-tasting elixir? Nothing helps us feel more hopeful about the world, and even about ourselves, than a good "belly-laugh."

Human History and the Rule of God

The story is told of a wise old Jewish rabbi who was informed that some persons said the messiah had already come. He made no reply but went to the window and looked out into the world full of hurting people. After a moment he turned and sadly shook his head. If the messiah had in fact come, he said, things would be very different; but apparently nothing had changed.

As we have seen already, human beings pursue the dream of forging an ideal community in history, and some have even confused this attempt with the true meaning of the kingdom or rule of God. Jesus did not preach a perfected human society, but a transformed reality that is a work of God, with our human cooperation.[11]

You and I cannot "bring in the kingdom" as some earlier and overly-optimistic generations thought. They thought that progress in education or science would usher in the new society where all people lived in goodwill and common respect. Too many tragedies have taught us that God's rule will not be instituted in this way. Our prayer and hope that "thy will be done on earth as it is in heaven" can make a significant difference, however.

Perhaps the rabbi could see no change in the squalid streets below his window, but are there no signs of the coming rule of God in our midst? A small rural congregation about fifty miles north of our home continues to kindle hope and faithfulness among its few members. On most Sundays, about twenty-five very diverse people gather for worship. Small children walk long distances to church, knowing that they will receive hugs and warmth that are often missing at home. The focus of Sunday school for them is not only learning the stories of God's love in the Bible, but also working on their reading skills and receiving encouragement about their school work. Older persons who can no longer attend have the services brought to them on various occasions. Two disabled adolescents feel accepted and at home among these friends—something they never experienced in the larger church of a nearby town.

The compassion of this small congregation keeps it alive when many nearby churches of similar size have been forced to shut their doors. This extended family realizes that it must stay together to survive, and in the process they are giving hope to many persons whose life circumstances could otherwise leave them hopeless. Granted, these signs of God's rule may be almost imperceptible to those looking for an overwhelming demonstration of the power of God, but did Jesus not use images of leaven, salt, and mustard-seed faith when he talked about the small beginnings of his realm?

When we look at our world, admittedly it is hard to see what difference persons of goodwill are making. Our downcast thoughts echo the third verse of Henry Wadsworth Longfellow's "I Heard the Bells on Christmas Day,"

And in despair I bowed my head:
"There is no peace on earth," I said,
For hate is strong, and mocks the song
Of peace on earth, good will to men.

Yet, there are small indications that God's way continues to provide leaven in human relationships and social structures. Just as crocuses signal the coming of spring, so do acts of transformation and compassion tell us, in the words of Longfellow's next verse, "The wrong shall fail, the right prevail." We cannot let ourselves be tempted by an "all or nothing" syndrome, however. Specifically, if we cannot cure the whole problem, why bother to work on a small dimension of it?

One of my close friends is a social worker who directs a program in our city to assist the homeless population. She recently informed me that her profession has one of the highest rates of persons who experience "burnout." These persons face problems of overwhelming proportions. Only those who are able to set realistic goals in one aspect of very complex social problems can see the difference that their efforts are making, enabling them to remain hopeful even though the task is far from complete. Those who attempt to be a "savior" for all are soon consumed with anger and make limited progress in meeting any concrete need.

One of my teaching colleagues speaks about authentic Christian commitment in a broken world in this folksy saying: "Each of us works somewhere in the vineyard; we need to discover where we are or need to be, and learn to be faithful there." Often we are staggered by the sheer complexity of human problems, and we hardly know where to begin. We must learn better how to work together in addressing both individuals and structures, for change cannot occur in one without change in the other.

Our world will be transformed primarily through changed hearts, which requires great patience. Even those of us who claim to be persons of faith know that we are always making the journey of conversion, and we are not yet what we shall be (I John 3:2). We must continue to act in hope, for it is a primary expression of our faith to work for the transformation of this world even as we sigh for the full establishing of God's reign. Human history finds its fullest meaning as we make present the redemption that is made possible through Jesus Christ.

Yet we know that many people die without ever receiving the justice of God, for the forces of good were not able, in their life-time, to defeat the evil structures that kept them in bondage.[12] For example, thousands of people have lost their lives in the years of the Palestinian intifada, that uprising of an oppressed people displaced from their land and denied many human rights by an intolerant government. So the question arises, "Is God's justice only for this life, or can we hope for it after death?" God's justice seems to demand eschatological resolution.

Resurrection and the Life Everlasting

As the early churches reflected on Jesus' promise to return and gather up the faithful, they began to question the fate of those who had died before his return. Where were those believers? Would they be able to share in the transformation promised to those who put their trust in Christ?

Questions like these from the churches in Corinth and Thessalonica prompted the Apostle Paul to formulate his under-standing of resurrection and the promise of life everlasting.[13] Until the resurrection of Jesus, religious experts argued whether or not persons could actually live after death. Although many were skeptical of the Christians' claim "He is risen, indeed," the debate about resurrection moved to a new level of intensity because of the testimony of the eyewitnesses about seeing him after he was raised.

To the believers in Thessalonica who had questions about those who had already died, Paul wrote a message of encouragement "so that you may not grieve as others do who have no hope" (1 Thess 4:13).

> For since we believe that Jesus died and rose again, even so, through Jesus, God will bring with him those who have died....For the Lord himself, with a cry of command, with the archangel's call and with the sound of God's trumpet, will descend from heaven, and the dead in Christ will rise first. Then we who are alive, who are left, will be caught up in the clouds together with them to meet the Lord in the air; and so we will be with the Lord forever. (1 Thess 4:15-17)

Paul assured those grief-stricken Christians that their departed loved ones were in the Lord's safe-keeping and were at no disadvantage because they had died before Christ's return for his own. Indeed, Paul went so far as to say that they actually enjoyed a greater privilege because they would precede in resurrection those still alive.[14]

To the Corinthians' question about the nature of the resurrection, Paul offered the most extensive description found in the New Testament.

> But someone will ask, "How are the dead raised? With what kind of body do they come?" Fool! What you sow does not come to life unless it dies....So it is with the resurrection of the dead. What is sown is perishable, what is raised is imperishable....If there is a physical body, there is also a spiritual body (1 Cor 15:35-36, 42, 44b).

Paul was not describing resuscitation, but a new mode of existence that can be described only as a "spiritual body." This suggests an embodied life that is not limited by the same constraints of the perishable physical body.[15] It is a new form of living that allows us the capacity for sharing fully in the life of God, as does the resurrected Christ.

Neither Paul nor other biblical writers suggest that human persons are by nature immortal. No, all of us will die, but those who place their trust in Christ will share in his resurrection. Participating in this transforming event, putting on immortality (1 Cor 15:54), is the Christian hope.

The Gospel of John perhaps is our best source for understanding the meaning of the life everlasting, or "eternal life," which is "that they may know you, the only true God, and Jesus Christ whom you have sent" (17:3). Thus, the quality of life that is called eternal can already begin. When we choose to follow Jesus Christ, we have already "passed from death to life" (John 5:24). Eternal life, therefore, has both a present and a future meaning. Although we have entered into eternal life through our confession of faith and baptism into Christ, we must remember that it also remains a promise for us, which will be fully completed in the future. John's Gospel also teaches that Jesus will raise believers "on the last day" (John 6:40; 11:25).

The assurance of resurrection has allowed countless persons to brave life-threatening tasks without fear. The hope of resurrection allows us both to value and risk our lives, for we realize that our lives can be entrusted to the safe-keeping of the one who first rose from the dead.

In earlier, perhaps more pious times, life on earth was viewed primarily as preparation for the life of heaven. Therefore, a person was to do as many meritorious acts as possible in order to enter into the full reward of heaven at the time of death. This idea led many persons to feel a great disdain for the things of this world, for they were simply a hindrance to the formation of the pure soul. Besides, life was often so harsh that death for the faithful seemed a welcome escape.

In contrast, our age does not think enough about what lies beyond death—until we or a loved one face a terminal illness or die suddenly. Even then, we give only passing attention to the brevity of our lives and our accountability to God. We seem more preoccupied with extending life than with proper preparation for death.

Thinking about eternal life in both its present and future dimensions can help "teach us to count our days, that we may gain a wise heart" (Ps 90:12). If we are really concerned about "quality of life," we will reflect on the character of life that we can live now in the strength of Christ.

A chaplain who works with senior adults has a wonderful description of aging: "The older you get, the more like yourself you become!"[16] The same could be said about our lives after death. If we live with open and generous hearts, our lives after death will only be a fuller, less hindered expression of that quality of life the Bible calls eternal. If we live in the death-like narcissism of self-preoccupation, however, our lives will have no room or appreciation for the shared life above. Thus, heaven and hell are two very different ultimate destinies for humankind.

Yet for those who put their trust in God and have already begun the journey of eternal life, we can face what lies beyond death with abiding hope and joyous expectation. Certainly we can expect a reunion with faithful loved ones and the opportunity to join in the praise of God with the saints of all times. Participating in an enduring friendship with God, we will finally realize the destiny for which we were created. Thanks be to God.

Endnotes

[1]John Macquarrie, *In Search of Humanity: A Theological and Philosophical Approach* (New York: Crossroad, 1993) 243.

[2]See Nicholas Lash, *A Matter of Hope* (Notre Dame IN: University of Notre Dame Press, 1982) 193.

[3]Catharina J. M. Halkes, *New Creation: Christian Feminism and the Renewal of the Earth* (Louisville KY: Westminster/John Knox Press, 1991) maintains that the eschatological vision of the Bible is essentially ecological.

[4]J. J. Collins, *The Apocalyptic Imagination: An Introduction to the Jewish Matrix of Christianity* (New York: Crossroad, 1984).

⁵Jim Garrison, *The Darkness of God: Theology after Hiroshima* (London: SCM Press Ltd., 1982) speaks of the "humanizing of the eschaton."

⁶See Douglas John Hall's exposition of church as this kind of community in *God and Human Suffering* (Minneapolis: Augsburg, 1986) chap. 5.

⁷See Ben Witherington, III, *Jesus, Paul, and the End of the World* (Downers Grove IL: InterVarsity Press, 1992) especially chaps. 20-21.

⁸Mary Grey, *Feminism Redemption and the Christian Tradition* (Mystic, CT: Twenty-Third Publications, 1990) stresses the significance of imagination in living out the Christian hope.

⁹I have been helped by Jürgen Moltmann's *The Theology of Play* (New York: Harper & Row, 1972). See also Regina Barreca, *They Used to Call Me Snow White . . . But I Drifted: Women's Strategic Use of Humor* (New York: Viking Press, 1991).

¹⁰See Howard Clinebell, *Well Being* (San Francisco: Harper San Francisco, 1992).

¹¹Paul McGlasson's book, *God the Redeemer: A Theology of the Gospel* (Louisville KY: Westminster/John Knox Press, 1993) 170, describes this community as "a provisional representation of redeemed humanity through faith in the crucified and risen Lord."

¹²The question of the reality and justice of God, which has dominated much of Jewish theology since the Holocaust, has been the focus of Elie Wiesel's work. In *Night* (New York: Avon, 1969) 55-56, Wiesel wrote: "I did not deny God's existence, but I doubted his absolute justice."

¹³See M. J. Harris, *Raised Immortal: Resurrection and Immorality in the New Testament* (Grand Rapids MI: Eerdmans, 1985).

¹⁴F. F. Bruce, *1 & 2 Thessalonians*, Word Biblical Commentary (Waco TX: Word Books, 1982): xxxvi-xxxix, offers a perceptive overview of eschatology at Thessalonica.

¹⁵Brian Hebbelethwaite, *The Christian Hope* (Grand Rapids MI: Eerdmans, 1984) 211, maintains "It is implausible to think of God's act of 'new creation' solely in terms of his holding in being a disembodied spirit in a society of pure spirits."

¹⁶I must credit my friend and sister in ministry, Libby Bellinger, for this memorable phrase.

LaVergne, TN USA
14 February 2010
173057LV00004B/2/P